W9-ARS-412

BELIZE

Reefs, Rain Forests, and Mayan Ruins

Dick Lutz

with Photographs by Mary Lutz

DIMI PRESS   Salem, Oregon

DIMI PRESS
3820 Oak Hollow Lane SE
Salem, Oregon 97302-4774

© 2005 by Dick Lutz

Library of Congress Cataloging-in-Publication Data

Lutz, Richard L., 1929-
  Belize:reefs, rain forests, and Mayan ruins/Dick Lutz.-- 1st ed.
      p.cm.
  Includes bibliographical references and index.
  ISBN-10: 0-931625-42-4 (trade pbk.)
  ISBN-13: 978-0-931625-42-8
  1. Lutz, Richard L., 1929---Travel--Belize.   2. Natural history--Belize. 3. Mayas--Belize. 4. Belize--Description and travel.   5. Belize--History. I. Title.
  F1444.3.L88 2005
  917.282'045--dc22
                          2005000574

Cover design by Bruce DeRoos

Photos of toucan & jaguar by Mason Fischer

Photo of Temple IV, Tikal by Craig Sholley

To the people of Belize

PREVIOUS BOOKS BY DICK LUTZ:

Feel Better! Live Longer! Relax!

The Running Indians

Komodo: The Living Dragon (co-authored with J. Marie Lutz)

Hidden Amazon

Patagonia: At the Bottom of the World

ACKNOWLEDGMENTS

Miriam Johnson of the Salem Public Library helped in gathering research materials. Janine Ebanks-Alpuche, Product Development Officer of the Belize Tourism Board, provided information about the history of tourism in Belize. Ray Hanson, author of The World Tree, graciously granted permission to use an excerpt from his book. Sherry Boyd, Tom Grasse, Jennifer Immel, and others of International Expeditions reviewed the manuscript and cover and provided additional help. Kathryn Staiano-Ross, with her scholarly knowledge of Belize, furnished much of the research material, gave good advice, and reviewed the manuscript. The Greater Victoria (Canada) Public Library also supplied some of the research material.

I owe a debt of gratitude to my fellow travelers on the tour group who helped make the trip enjoyable as well as educational. Dick & Lola Brett, Ray & Diane Luety, Ron & Esther Spencer, Golda Doyle, Becky Miller, and Barry Quinn are all neat people and, in a sense, should be considered co-authors of this book.

Although most of the photographs in this book were taken by my wife, Mary, those that were not are credited to the photographer or owner.

CONTENTS

INTRODUCTION

Belize is the least populated Central American nation. Until its full independence in 1981 it was called British Honduras and was a colony of Great Britain. From 1964 to 1981 the country was essentially self-governing with Britain retaining responsibility only for foreign affairs, internal security, and defense. Actually, the name Belize was adopted in 1973 in anticipation of its independence. Belize remains a member of the British Commonwealth of Nations. This means little except that a Governor General is the Queen's representative. This person is a Belizean and is selected by the Belize government.

There are several theories as to the origin of the name Belize. It may come from the Mayan word belix meaning muddy water. Some think it is a derivation of the word belikin meaning "land that looks toward the east (or seas)." A local historian thinks the word came from the Spanish version of the name Wallace, the Scottish warrior. The weakness of this argument is that there is no proof that Wallace ever visited what is now Belize. A fourth theory is that the name is of African origin. The fact is, no one knows for sure.

The nation is about the same size as Massachusetts, and is only 174 miles long and 68 miles wide. Along with Costa Rica it may be the most peaceful country in Central America (and perhaps in all of Latin America). Civil wars, violence, and repression have dogged Guatemala, El Salvador, Nicaragua, and Panama but not Belize.

Belize lies on the Caribbean and is bordered on the north and northwest by Mexico, and on the west and south by Guatemala.

It has a subtropical climate with annual rainfall ranging from 55 inches in the northern part of the country to 180 in the south. The average temperature varies somewhat with 75° F in January and 81° F in July. Generally, the dry season is between November and May with the rainy season June to November. Rain does occur in the dry season but it is usually brief.

Belize is an amazingly diverse country both in its land and its people. In the north, the land consists of low-lying plains that are frequently swampy. In the south, the Maya Mountains overlook a narrow coastal plain. To the east lie the barrier reef and the cayes and the Turneffe Islands, all in the clear waters of the Caribbean.

The most striking geographical feature of Belize is the barrier reef some ten to twenty miles offshore. This is the longest barrier reef in the western hemisphere. Fringing this reef are some 175 cayes (pronounced "kees") or islets. Due to the shallow, clear water some of the best skindiving and snorkeling spots in the world are located off this reef.

The wildlife population of most of Central America has been decimated over the years. But Belize is different. Jaguars, tapirs, crocodiles, and exotic bird species can still be found here. The fact that the nation is underdeveloped and underpopulated means that the wildlife has had room to survive. Not that Belize is a Garden of Eden paradise—but relative to other countries in Central America it is a stable, peaceful place with an abundance of nature's blessings.

The population of Belize is as diverse as its geography. The ethnicity is as follows: Mestizo 48.7%, Creole 24.9%, Mayan 10.6%, Garifuna 6.1%, and other 9.7%.

The existence of Mayan ruins and the remains of the Mayan culture make Belize a fascinating place to visit. To understand the ruins better it is advisable to know the periods of Mayan history. These are generally accepted by the archeologists and other scientists who study the Mayans. They are as follows:

Preclassic period — (600 BC–250 AD)

Early classic period — (250–448 AD)

Middle classic period — (448–682 AD)

Late classic period — (682–909 AD)

In addition, some writers mention a Terminal classic period dating after 830 AD. The term Postclassic is also used. As you visit the Mayan ruins you will find almost all of the artifacts and structures classified according to the above breakdown. It will enhance your experience if you remember these periods.

Hurricanes have been a problem. Between 1978 and 1997 there were no destructive hurricanes but then came Hurricane Mitch in 1998, Keith in 2000, and Iris in 2001. The most destructive was the 1931 hurricane and Hattie in 1961. Hattie was so destructive, particularly in low-lying Belize City, that the government built the new city of Belmopan and moved the capital there. The most damaging hurricanes have occurred in the months of August, September, and October. The hurricane warning system has become quite sophisticated so you can be assured that your guide will get you to shelter if necessary.

Tour groups conducted by International Expeditions in Belize vary in size from six to sixteen. If the group consists of few travelers, then the guide will also be the driver of the bus. Otherwise, there are either two guides, one of whom is the driver, or a driver is hired to accompany the guide. Our group was fortunate to have two guides.

GUIDES

Our primary guide was a smiling Scotsman named Martin Meadows. Martin handled all arrangements smoothly and was very knowledgeable about everything. He had many stories about his adventures in Africa as well as Belize. Trained in forestry, Martin works at the Belize Botanical Gardens.

The driver of our very comfortable bus was also a certified guide. A native Belizean, Nathan Forbes was equally knowledgeable about birds, animals, plants, the Mayans, the Belize government, and customs. He also knew a lot about the history of Belize and was a very nice guy.

The Coat of Arms of Belize

The motto - "Sub Umbra Florero" - means "Under the shade I flourish."

Central America

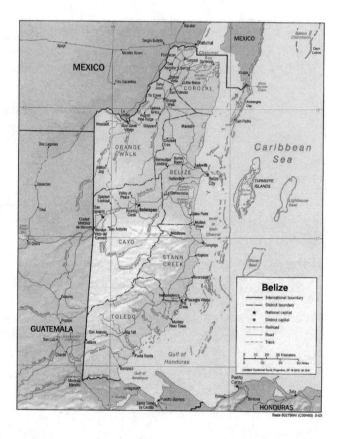

Base 802759AI (C00493) 2-03

CHAPTER I

Expedition

(Day 1)

Belize City

L anding at the small Belize International Airport in Belize City our group soon got together after we all arrived from vartous cities. Driving around the little oval loop in front of the airport, we immediately encountered several interesting birds. Most were perched on the fence surrounding some army barracks.

It was pleasing to observe that the signs were in English even though Belize is an obviously tropical country. In fact, Belize is the only Central American country where English is the official language. Many other languages are spoken, the most common of which are Spanish and Creole.

After all eleven of us were assembled, we started off to the northwestern part of the country. The bus was a modern twenty-passenger vehicle. With our group this left plenty of room for our luggage. The bus contained a cooler that always seemed to be full of water and soft drinks.

The first several miles of our trip were on a paved road through a rural area. The terrain was flat and rather colorless. I guess you'd call it savannah. There were a few rather malnourished-looking trees. The soil here is very poor, and as we were to learn, there is consequently very little dirt farming. As we drove north the countryside became more forested but we saw fewer and fewer people.

Boat ride

After about an hour we came to the New River (which we had previously crossed.) Before getting into the boat I tried in vain to talk with a Mennonite farmer who was standing by the little pier. He seemed friendly enough but apparently spoke only German.

At the New River we got into a boat and, for about forty-five minutes, went up the river. This boat trip took us through a jungle and during the whole trip we saw no boats, people, or any sign of civilization. We felt like we were deep into the recesses of the world!

Before dark fell, a planet emerged in the sky. Still daylight, the planet shone like a tiny sun in the blue sky. I don't recall ever seeing such a sight.

The river opened out into the New River Lagoon and we landed at the lodge. Dark comes quickly in the tropics and, although it was not yet seven o'clock, it was pitch dark. We were led to our respective cabins that had been previously assigned.

New River

New River Lagoon

Lamanai Outpost Lodge

The lodge is perched on a hillside and looks out on the New River Lagoon. The lagoon is described as varying in length between 17 and 28 miles depending on the amount of water in it. It is several miles across. Despite the fact that it is located deep in the jungle there is an airstrip nearby. In addition, the lodge has telephone and e-mail service, electricity, and hot and cold running water. All the rooms are in individual cabins and are equipped with ceiling fans, hardwood floors, and attractive furnishings. The roofs are thatched and there are lush tropical plants everywhere including huge palm trees. Truly a delightful spot.

The staff is helpful but one member is a bit unusual. He was a member of a Mennonite community until he married a girl who wasn't. He was immediately ejected from the community.

Dinner

An excellent meal was served in the open-air dining room shortly after our arrival. We had a choice of shrimp ceviche, chicken picatta, or a plantain and fish stew. Dessert was chocolate cake or ice cream.

(Day 2)

Morning birdwalk

The area immediately surrounding the lodge is considered to be one of the best bird-watching sites in Central America. Those of us who had risen for the early morning walk this beautiful day walked slowly along a dirt road for a half-mile or so. The trees were definitely taller in this area as opposed to the area we came through yesterday. One side of the road was an impenetrable jungle. A brief shower fell on the return walk but we dried up quickly. The bird sightings were as varied and plentiful as any birder could wish.

Ruins of Lamanai

The area of the Lamanai Mayan Ruins (or Archaeological Reserve) is about 4.6 sq km or 1.8 sq mi. Some 720 structures have been identified in the Reserve but only 70 have been excavated to varying degrees.

It was not until 1978 that it was realized that Lamanai means "submerged crocodile." This name was recorded by Franciscan missionaries in the 17th century and is definitely the original Maya name although it has been spelled in various ways. There are a number of crocodile representations at the site including figurine headdresses, vessel decorations, and the headdress of a twelve foot high limestone mask on the platform of a sixth century temple.

Walking the short distance (perhaps half a mile) to the Mayan sites, we came across the ruins of two Spanish churches that had been built on this site in the 15th and 16th centuries. Lamanai was occupied from 800 BC until 1850 A.D. Archaeologists have determined that maize was cultivated at this site as early as 1500 B.C. Little is known about what happened at this site until about 500 B.C. The earliest pottery fragments date from this period. Lamanai was occupied later than most Mayan sites and was conquered by the Spanish.

Although the Lamanai community never really collapsed as did Tikal and other sites, this was probably due to the fact that it was never conquered by enemies (until the Spanish.) The river and lagoon on which it borders yielded fish and turtles to keep its people from starving.

As is true at most Mayan ruins, the various structures have been built over, sometimes several times. For instance, within the sixth century masked temple was discovered a small, well-preserved temple dating from about 100 B.C. Also, the High Temple (known as Structure N10-43) has been modified several times, the last time around 600 A.D. It is thought that the fact that the later structures are smaller and less spectacular means that there was a lessening supply of labor and that society became progressively less hierarchical as time passed. More information on the changes in Maya culture over the centuries can be found in Chapter IV, History of the Mayans.

From the ruins of the Spanish churches we walked about a quarter-mile to the Mayan ruins themselves. We walked through a jungle-like area and along stone paths. Then we had an outdoor breakfast spread for us by the people from the Lodge who brought it by bus. It consisted of a Spanish omelette and fruit. It was an excellent breakfast in a spectacular setting.

We then walked a little further in the Lamanai area to the small museum where the guide explained the different periods of the Mayan empire. The artifacts in the museum were mainly broken pots that had been restored. They showed the differing artistic styles in the different periods. The explanations by the guide made it an interesting exhibit.

The area around the center structures had, at times, been primarily residential. The usage of specific areas changed over time with formerly residential areas being converted to ceremonial grounds and vice versa.

We continued to walk through the forest until we came to the previously mentioned Mask Temple. The large mask has a roof over it as it is made of a relatively soft sandstone that would erode away in the rain.

Along the way the guides identified the plants and trees as well as the birds. Throughout the trip Martin and Nathan did a superb job of identification of the flora and fauna. They also explained about this temple.

Proceeding on through the jungle—examining plants, spotting birds—we came to the High Temple (Structure NC10-43.) Two of our group climbed to the top of the temple while the rest of us watched. The temple is so steep that a rope has been provided to aid climbers. It is nearly 33 meters (108 feet) in height and is the largest Preclassic structure in the entire Maya area, not just in Belize.

Moving on to the ball court, past an area in front of the High Temple, we observed the flat ground between two mounds facing each other. Later in this book, Mayan ball courts will be dealt with at greater length.

The group went next to the Mayan ruins known as the Royal Complex. One of the pyramid-shaped buildings of the Royal Complex is called the Jaguar Temple because of its decorations. After admiring and photographing these structures we returned by bus to the lodge. The ruins are laid out in a more or less circular pattern and thus the return trip was brief.

The previous occupants of the Lamanai site include not only Maya of all periods but also Spanish clergy, British sugar cane growers, and even Chinese workers! The first amateur archeologist to visit the site was in 1917 but serious and professional work did not begin until 1974. This work was done by David Pendergast of the Royal Ontario Museum, Canada..

After lunch the group listened to a lecture and slide show presented by the Lamanai Research Center concerning

High Temple at Lamanai

the native wildlife with emphasis on the local crocodile, the Murrelet's crocodile. They eat mostly apple snails but also have been known to eat fish, turtles, and even catch birds by leaping out of the water.

The Lamanai Field Research Center (LFRC) conducts a variety of projects in biological science and anthropology. A number of outside sources support this research and some of the revenue comes from the Lamanai Outpost Lodge. Thus, our stay at the Lamanai Outpost Lodge helped support the Research Center. Following this presentation some of the group returned to the Mayan ruins for another look before dinner.

Dinner consisted of linguini or a shrimp dish with a dessert of key lime pie. The meal was excellent as were all the meals at Lamanai Outpost Lodge.

Night Spotlight Safari

This turned out to be a fascinating excursion. Clambering into a boat with all the seats facing forward, we motored through the New River Lagoon and up the New River. The boat was equipped with a movable searchlight as well as two fixed and powerful lights beaming ahead. The eagle-eyed boat driver continually scanned the surrounding jungle with the searchlight. His ability to locate wildlife was uncanny. There were several remarkable birds spotted. To our delight the birds did not fly away (as long as the spotlight wasn't directly on them). In addition we spotted a basilisk lizard (also known as a "Jesus Christ lizard"). Unfortunately, it was in a tree so we did not see it walk on water (the characteristic that gives it its second name). We also saw three Morelet's crocodiles and an iguana.

Taking a minute to turn out all the lights, the motor, and silencing any other sound, we enjoyed the many stars and planets in the night sky and the faint sounds of the jungle. Quite an experience!

(Day 3)

After a delicious breakfast of French toast and scrambled eggs, we were given the option of traveling back to the New River landing either by bus or by boat. From the landing we proceeded by bus to the Belize Zoo. The bus ride was through Mennonite country and we passed several horse-drawn buggies driven by men with flat hats and farmer's overalls. Most had beards. The women wore long dresses and most had bonnets or scarfs over their heads. The children were mostly dressed like miniature men or women. All were unsmiling but they would usually return a waved greeting.

A few times we took out cameras to take their pictures but when the Mennonites noticed this they immediately turned their backs. They didn't want to be photographed. This day was Sunday. When we passed a simple Mennonite church, there were thirty or so horse and buggy rigs drawn up in the "parking lot." It was a picturesque scene

Crooked Tree

On the way we stopped briefly at the Crooked Tree Wildlife Sanctuary. Our bus crossed the causeway to the little village of Crooked Tree. The lagoon on either side of the causeway was alive with flocks of water birds. Those of the group interested in birding got off and Martin set up his spotting scope for a better look. The non-birders stayed on the bus as Nathan drove it into the village. This rural community is called Crooked Tree because it is the home of many cashew trees which have a very crooked shape.

There is a Cashew Festival here held every year on the first weekend in May. This consists of live music, storytelling, and eating, especially cashews. The Festival was started in 1992 by International Expeditions, particularly by Tom Grasse, Director of Marketing. This was done to increase tourism and help the economic development of Crooked Tree. This is an example of how this tour company aids the local economy wherever they go.

We drove around town asking where we could buy some cashews, finally finding three pounds in an old house. We bought them all, apparently getting the last of the previous season's crop. After picking up the birders we proceeded toward the Belize Zoo. Before visiting the zoo we had lunch at a restaurant called 'Cheers!'

Belize Zoo

The only zoo in Belize was started in 1983 by Sharon Mattola an American woman who has been a biologist and a circus performer in her varied career. The original residents of the zoo were wild animals which had been used in a documentary film about tropical forests.

Ms. Mattola still is the Director of the Zoo. Several American celebrities have supported the zoo's development. The architect who designed the current zoo donated his services and several foreign zoos have contributed animals and birds.

Also, International Expeditions assisted the zoo in its early stages. This was indirectly made possible by Ms. Mattola who was an early guide for the tour company. Reportedly, she took her earnings from IE and used them to support the zoo while she lived on the tips given to her by tourists.

After the zoo was established, it was soon realized that Belizeans were not familiar with the different species of wildlife in their own country. This discovery resulted in the comittment to develop the little zoo into a wildlife education center.

It exhibits only animals indigenous to Belize—with over 125 of them at present. The animals are given to the zoo for rehabilitation, born at the zoo, or sent as gifts from other zoos. One of the most interesting features of the zoo is the fact that the signs are often amusing (see photos.)

For a small zoo it is outstanding. It has large enclosures for all its animals, each a jungle-like environment. Yet zoo visitors can easily observe the animals Some of the enclosures have raised walkways for better observation by visitors. The exceedingly rare and very impressive harpy eagle is, perhaps, its most outstanding exhibit. The harpy is the largest eagle in existence and is extinct in the wild in Belize.

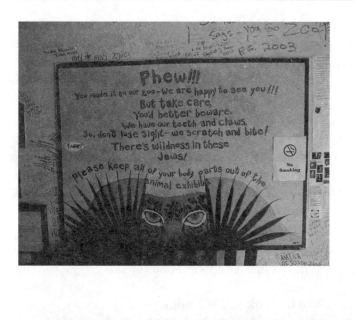

If you're in the mood for somethin' funky...
Then look up here at we SPIDER MONKEYS!
We swing through the trees with the greatest
of ease! When missing a thumb.....
BRACHIATION is a BREEZE!!

The Belize Zoo has also done a great deal for conservation in Belize. Although open to tourists (and on the International Expeditions tour) the zoo has its major impact on the Belizeans themselves. Families, individuals, and school groups are constantly visiting the zoo and thus the zoo's conservation message is spreading to the Belizean culture.

Many environmental groups, most of them from the United States, have played a major role in the conservation efforts in Belize. Several U. S. Audubon societies, including the Massachusetts and Florida groups have founded the Belize Audobon Society.

Traveling to Pook's Hill Lodge

On our way to our next overnight at Pook's Hill, we detoured through the capitol city, Belmopan. This is a charming and well laid out city with spacious roadways, attractive buildings, and lots of parks. Traveling on to Pook's Hill Lodge we found ourselves in an increasingly jungle-like area. As we progressed the road got narrower and narrower. When we turned off the main highway on to the road to the lodge we traversed a section with ferns some twenty to thirty feet high. The plants loomed over the bus like sails over a ship. As one of our group commented, "This is what I expected Belize to look like."

Pook's Hill Lodge

This beautiful resort is located on a cleared and grassy hill surrounded by jungle. It is set in the foothills of the Maya Mountains. The individual thatched-roof cabins are clustered around a Mayan archeological site (see photos.) The main lodge is at the bottom of the hill and features a spacious open-air lounge with a bar and an interesting little library. On the floor below the lounge is the dining room.

Although not considered a major Mayan site, the three small mounds have yielded twelve graves of ordinary Mayans. The residential complex dates mainly from the ninth and tenth centuries. The excavation work has been done under the auspices of the government and with the help of volunteer labor from foreign countries.

The fact that a private lodge surrounds an officially controlled archeological site is an example of Belize's enlightened policy of non-governmental/governmental cooperation.

While walking around the lawn we were shown the black orchid, the national flower of Belize. This small, dainty flower is actually dark purple (see photo.)

The name, Pook's Hill, comes from a book by Rudyard Kipling. The owners of the lodge, Ray and Vicki Snaddon, were reading Kipling to their young daughter at the time when they needed to choose a name for their lodge. The young girl suggested Pook's Hill. Also, Puuc is a common Mayan name so the name has a double meaning.

Ray breeds iguanas that are indigenous to the area. This, too, stems from an interest of his daughter. As a child (she is now away at college) she became interested in the fact that many iguanas were coming into the Pook's Hill clearing to lay their eggs. Her father brought in some sand to make it easier for them to dig their nests.

Since snakes, rats, and other wildlife like to eat the lizard eggs, Ray built a small, heated enclosure for them. The hatchery is temperature-controlled. As is true of many reptiles the degree of warmth of the eggs determines the sex of the iguana. If the temperature is more than 31°C (82°F) the emerging animal will be male. If the temperature is less than that the lizard will be female. After hatching, the young iguanas are kept in another enclosure for a year or so before being released into the wild. There had been a release of about fifty of the lizards shortly before we arrived.

Ray has discovered that many of the iguanas (perhaps 50%) return to the spot where they were hatched to lay their own eggs.

Ray and Vicki are assisted in the operation of the Pook's Hill Lodge by a young Belgian couple who proved to be quite helpful. One of the remarkable facts about this

Pook's Hill Mayan site

Pook's Hill cabins

lodge is that they heat the water by burning the nuts of the cohune palm tree. This is an old-fashioned process that probably stems from Mayan days.

Among the many features of this lodge is the availability of e-mail.

Night walk in jungle

Following a good dinner of pork, rice, broccoli, and carrot cake some of us took a night walk into the jungle. This walk extended only a half-mile or so but was well worth it. One member of our party spotted an armadillo and we saw a number of unusual insects including a long line of leafcutter ants carrying their green burdens. These creatures are most active at night and, on this occasion, were filing down a huge tree trunk.

We also spotted a lizard that looked much like the basilisk but was considerably smaller. Nathan said that it was an 'old man lizard.' This is the common name for the Helmeted Basilisk. We saw no snakes—apparently they are spotted only about 20% of the time.

Iguana   Ray Snaddon

Iguana enclosure

(Day 4)

Green Hills Butterfly Farm

On setting out for this morning's adventure we again drove through the virtual tunnel of overhanging ferns with strangler figs and othr attractive vines and trees in the jungle. Also we observed many wildflowers and fascinating birds flitting among the tree branches. Part of the road we traveled on was through another picturesque Mennonite farm community.

The butterfly farm is a breeding center with an interpretive focus. A Dutch couple, Jan Meerman and Tineke Boomsma, run the operation. We enjoyed an outdoor lunch of chicken, jasmine rice, and fried plantains, with a tomato and onion salad. There were cookies for dessert. A brief lecture from Jan on some of the local flowers followed. We toured the butterfly breeding enclosure and a knowledgeable young woman explained the breeding process to us.

The farm raises several different kinds of butterflies and the pupas are shipped to zoos and other destinations in the United States and Canada. Two of their markets are the Milwaukee Zoo and the Houston Zoo. The various species of butterflies need different plants on which to lay their eggs. The eggs of each type of butterfly are unique and are collected in different ways. Evev the pupas are dissimilar and have their own incubation periods. This was an enthralling visit.

Jan Meerman, Green Hills Butterfly Farm

Butterfly breeding explained

Returning to Pook's Hill we had several hours of free time before dinner. An option this afternoon was to visit the cave at Rio Frio.

There are many caves in Belize. The ancient Mayans used them as a source of fresh water in dry periods. Also, caves were used for religious and ceremonial purposes. Clay pots full of grain were sometimes stored in the caves, At times they were used as burial chambers,. It is believed the caves were untouched for some 2,000 years. Then, in the 1960s they began to be researched and mapped. Today over 300 caves have been explored and charted.

Dinner consisted of beef, potatoes, fried eggplant, rice, beans, and homemade coconut ice cream.

(Day 5)

Ruins of Xunantunich

After breakfast we packed up and rode for about an hour. We went through San Ignacio, a relatively prosperous city. Arriving at the town of San Jose Succotz, we left the bus and walked on to a little ferry that crossed the Mopan River.

A hand crank that pulled it along a cable propelled the ferry. Our bus was too big to go on the ferry although cars did. On the other side of the river a van was waiting to take us about a mile up a hill to the magnificent ruins of Xunantunich (Stone Woman.)

El Castillo, Xunantunich

View from El Castillo, Xunantunich

This is an impressive site. Some of us climbed part way up El Castillo, the main monument. This pyramid rises some 130 feet above the main plaza and provides an impressive panoramic view over the forested area of western Belize and also Guatemala.

Xunantunich (Shoo-NAN-too-niche) was a major ceremonial center for the Maya. It flourished during the Classic Period. Containing six major plazas and more than twenty-five temples and palaces, the outstanding feature of interest is the reconstructed frieze on the side of the lower temple. At one time, El Castillo was considered to be the largest man-made structure in Belize.

Exploration of this site began in 1894 and numerous amateur archeologists have worked it since. Perhaps because it is close to a populous area, Xunantunich has been looted more than most Maya sites. Many of the artifacts from here are in museums in Europe or have been lost forever.

However, the site has an informative visitors' center which include some fine examples of stelae (engraved stone pillars.) Martin had witnessed some of the excavation done on these ruins and told some interesting anecdotes about that process.

It rained briefly while we were at this site but it was warm enough that we dried off quickly. After visiting Xunantunich the group returned to San Ignacio where we had lunch at an outdoor restaurant. Martin lives in

San Ignacio and we stopped by his house to pick up his wife and two young children to take them downtown.

After leaving San Ignacio we drove to the Guatemalan border. The checks at both the Belize side and the Guatemalan side consisted only of showing our passports and other papers that had previously been given to us. The area between the two countries, perhaps 100 yards across, is known as 'No Man's Land.'

Entering Guatemala

Re-entering our bus, we drove into Guatemala. The difference between the two countries was immediately apparent. First of all, the Guatemala road was in terrible condition although it later got better. The Belizean road to the border was paved and in good shape. The Guatemalan thoroughfare was muddy and the driver had to be careful not to slip off the road. Also, there were many large trucks on the road in Guatemala. We seldom saw a truck in Belize (except outside of the sugar cane processing plant.)

The poverty of the households we passed, both in towns and in rural areas, was evident. Although we had driven past some poor homes in Belize, they were not nearly as bad off as those we saw in Guatemala. As we went along, the road improved but there were still frequent potholes. The road signs were now in Spanish.

About 5:15 we arrived at the Tikal Inn, which is inside the Tikal National Park. It had taken us nearly three hours to travel some sixty miles.

Tikal Inn

The Hotel Tikal Inn is a gorgeous resort located within a ten-minute walk of the center of the Mayan ruins. It is at the edge of the jungle. Our rooms bordered a large swimming pool, and the lawn and gardens were very well maintained and beautiful. The rooms all had a ceiling fan but electricity was only on for about an hour in the early morning and for about four hours in the evening. Since we were gone most of the day this was not a problem. Access to e-mail is available next door at the Jaguar Inn.

The dinner, although adequate, was not up to the standard set by our previous meals on this expedition.

(Day 6)

Ruins of Tikal

On this day we experienced what was the most impressive stop on our tour. Having visited most of the major Mayan sites in Mexico, I was still unprepared for the grandeur of Tikal. It is arguably the most spectacular Mayan site.

The ruins are set in the center of the Tikal National Park which is an impressive facility in and of itself. The 200

square–mile preserve contains more than 2,000 plant species, more than 300 different kinds of birds, and 54 different species of animals. The animals, although not tame, are relatively comfortable around people. We saw kinkajou, grey fox, monkeys (both howler and spider), coatimundi, and agouti.

One of the most beautiful birds we saw was the ocellated turkey. This bird looks much like our North American turkey in size and shape, but it is quite colorful. A number of them were "hanging out" a short distance from the Hotel Tikal Inn, and we had a close-up look at them, even while they were mating.

The roads and paths in the park are well maintained and Tikal National Park would be worth visiting even if the Mayan ruins were not its centerpiece. But the ruins are magnificent!

Tikal is probably the best understood of the hundreds of Mayan sites. The many artifacts, friezes, stelae, and decorated buildings that have been found here tell a fascinating story. Tikal came into existence in the Preclassic period (600 BC to 250 AD) when the villages in the area grew and became towns. It grew throughout the entire Classic period (250–909 AD) In the Early classic period (250–448 AD) it rose to its preeminent position in the Mayan world primarily through the subjugation of the surrounding districts.

During the Middle classic period (448–682 AD) Tikal declined somewhat due to outside military pressure.

Then it enjoyed a resurgence in the Late classic period (682–909 AD), which left it first in the panoply of Mayan cities. Sometime in the Terminal classic period (after 830 AD) the city simply stopped. The Maya abandoned it and wandered away. Exactly why this termination occurred is not known for certain and remains the subject of considerable speculation among scientists.

The early settlers in the region probably came there because of its abundant flint deposits. Also it was attractive because of its location on the western edge of seasonal swamps while it was still on a rugged escarpment that dominated the local landscape. The latter offered a significant defensive position.

By 600 BC the inhabitants built houses of stick walls and thatched roofs and farmed the countryside. There were not more than a few dozen of them. It is not known where they came from or what they called themselves and their villages. It is known that they beheaded at least one person. This tiny and unremarkable group of simple farmers was the beginning of a great city that lasted fifteen hundred years.

Ceramic dating techniques are the best indicator of an object's age. The chief tool that archeologists use is radiocarbon dating, which, although not precise, gives results within 100 years. Radiocarbon dating measures the rate of radioactive decay in organic material like bones and charcoal.

The information about these people is largely gained from the pottery shards that have been found, mostly in middens. The pottery from the Preclassic period is simple and with little decoration. The style of the pottery and other artifacts also gives some clue as to the date of the object.

The earlier settlers in Central America were nomadic, but those who settled in what was to become the Tikal area began tilling the soil. These early farmers cleared the land of trees by chopping them down with axes. The axes used were made with stone blades created with the local flint.

The farmers allowed the downed forest to dry during the dry season and then burned off the land. This not only effectively cleared the land but also enriched the soil with potassium.

This technique of burning off the milpas (plots of land) is still used today in parts of Central America. It is usually referred to as slash-and-burn agriculture. The problem with this type of farming is that the soil is depleted of its nutrients (except for potassium) in two or three seasons. As long as there was plenty of land available this wasn't much of a problem. Farmers just moved to another plot of land after the first got worn out.

Maize (a type of corn) was the primary product of the soil although chiles, avocadoes, beans, squash, tomatoes, and various herbs were also grown. Chocolate, the product of the cacao tree, was also developed and the cacao beans were even used as currency.

The maize was utilized as food in many different ways. It could be dried and ground and made into dough for tamales or tortillas. The dough could be dissolved in water to make a drink called pozole or boiled to make a gruel called atole.

There were apparently three hamlets that grew into Tikal. By 500 BC trade was increasing and the hamlets grew in number and in size. The first permanent buildings at Tikal were influenced in design by the Olmec culture to the west. Around 200–100 BC structures of cut-stone masonry were built with walls of masonry and roofs of perishable thatch. They were plastered and painted inside and out.

These were tombs that were built over in subsequent years and were eventually decorated with sculpted and painted friezes. These structures became what is known today as the North Acropolis. For several hundred years they were used as burial tombs and shrines for revered members of the community.

In these early centuries Tikal was becoming increasingly socially stratified. Persons buried in the more elaborate crypts were heads of families and lineages. Some families were gaining in importance. Power became concentrated in a few bold leaders who were wealthy enough and powerful enough to encourage (or force) the poorer people to build shrines and other public works.

Some of those public works were the massive reservoirs carved out of bedrock. Water was a problem in Tikal so these reservoirs were dug to help solve that problem. It was about this time that the Mayans began the use of raised fields for agriculture. This technique enabled the community to intensify the raising of crops to sustain an increasing population.

The Lost World Complex was constructed around this time. This pyramid contained, in addition to a shrine, an astronomical feature. Its orientation allowed for the calculation of the equinox and solstice and was the first observation that formed the basis of a solar calendar. The Lost World Complex was completed about 1 AD. At a height of 100 feet it was one of the most massive structures in Precolumbian America. There were other similar structures near Tikal but none as grand as this pyramid.

The population of Tikal grew dramatically during this time and thatched huts spread across the surrounding terrain. A major event may have caused Tikal's population to increase markedly—the eruption of the distant volcano, Ilopango. Although a tremendous blast, Ilopango was so far away from Tikal that it did no damage. However, it caused many people to move to Tikal.

The massive volcanic eruption had devastated a large area, including a densely inhabited Mayan site called Chalchuapa in present-day El Salvador. Thousands of people were killed and Chalchuapa was buried under two feet of ash. Close to the volcanic cone the ash was 170 feet thick. Although not directly affected by the eruption, the skies over Tikal were probably darkened by the volcanic particles, and there is indication of an increase in the amount of rainfall.

With the development of hieroglyphic writing, and supplemented by their decorative art, the people of Tikal began to record their history and development. The first of these records can be dated to the year 292 AD. The records run continuously for more than 600 years, giving an unprecedented look at the history of Tikal.

It would be 1,000 years before a Precolumbian people would leave so clear a record of their times.

In the museum at Tikal can be found Stela 29,which was discovered by an archeological team from the University of Pennsylvania in 1958. This stela contains hieroglyphs that indicate the earliest date in recorded Tikal history— July 8, 292 AD.

Stela 29 also depicts an early ruler of Tikal, whose name was later established as Foliated Jaguar. He was called a Kalomte, a royal designation equivalent to king. His father has been called Jaguar's Paw, but the founder of the dynastic line is known as First Step Shark. These names have been given by scientists, either as descriptions of the glyphs of these rulers or as literal translations from the Mayan.

It is not known when First Step Shark lived, but it is clear that his people revered him. The line of succession from the dynasty he established leads forward until 790 AD when his 29th successor ruled. Some of these rulers were queens, but most were kings.

Although the North Acropolis remained the burial place of kings and queens, the Central Acropolis was the seat of government. At least one of the rulers also maintained his palace in this structure.

Rather than attempting to document the various rulers and the political turmoil of their reigns, suffice it to say that there were repeated indications of wars, changes in the economy, and various other upheavals. Other books detail what is known about these disruptions. Perhaps best of all is John Montgomery's **TIKAL: An Illustrated History of the Ancient Maya Capital.** An excellent guidebook available on site is **TIKAL: A Handbook of the Ancient Maya Ruins** by William R. Coe.

There is one incident that is well described in the literature. The twenty-first ruler in the line of succession from First Step Shark led the army of Tikal into an attack on Caracol, a Maya site in southern Belize. This occurred in 556 AD. Caracol was heavily damaged and many captives were taken back to Tikal, presumably as slaves.

Then six years later Caracol, with help from the neighboring Mayan city of Naranjo, viciously attacked

Tikal. This attack was much more devastating than the earlier one. Monuments and temples were destroyed. Tikal was burned to the ground.

Stelae had been erected regularly for centuries in Tikal but now none were put up for 150 years. No major buildings were begun for at least 75 years. Scholars have dubbed this period "the hiatus." During this period Tikal was only one of several Mayan cities under a central control.

In the Late classic period (682 AD to 909 AD) Tikal flowered again. The North Acropolis saw even more grandiose projects, particularly tombs, and the ball court was built at this time. A strong ruler solidified the ascendancy of Tikal over many other Mayan areas and married a woman from one of the important neighboring tribes. Temple II was built at this time as a memorial to this woman who died at a young age. Indeed, the only representation of a woman that is to be found in central Tikal is located on a frieze of this temple.

Jasaw Kaan K'awil, the ruler who resurrected Tikal, lived some eighty years and died in about 734 AD. His son had Temple I built in his memory. This huge edifice was probably painted red originally. One can easily imagine how its stunning crest would have blazed over the city for miles. Temple I is one of the most spectacular pyramids of the Precolumbian era and inaugurated the last great building splurge of Tikal.

Temple I, Tikal

The son then built Temple IV as his own funeral monument. Temple IV is the tallest structure ever built at Tikal. This ruler, Yik'in Kaan K'awil, also conquered nearby cities. It is believed that succession passed from this ruler to either his younger brother or his son. Although many facts about Tikal are known there also are many that aren't.

Temple IV turned out to be the crowning achievement of the rulers of Tikal. In all of their thousand years of architecture nothing had been so overwhelmingly grand. By the time Temple IV was built there was little, if any, jungle left in the area. Looking out over Tikal from the top of this magnificent pyramid one would have seen thousands of residential sites around the central downtown core. The houses would have ranged from simple, thatched-roof huts, to stone buildings with multiple rooms and courtyards, to the palaces of the rulers. Today we saw mostly jungle. It has returned over the centuries. Several of the tallest structures emerge from the forest canopy.

After the construction of Temple IV, the building of monuments and pyramids continued but the quality and richness of the decorations began to decline. The Mayan world was waning at this time but Tikal may have been one of the last cities to realize this fact. The last ceremonial burial of an important person occurred around 780 AD.

Temple III was completed between 820 and 830 with the

last record of a ruler in 869. The last reference to Tikal in any Mayan inscription was in 889 AD.

At Tikal people simply moved away leaving perhaps only four or five hundred continuing to live among the ruins. Garbage accumulated on the Central Acropolis, buildings fell into disrepair and some collapsed. Debris lay where it fell, and the starving survivors took to eating the flesh of dead relatives. By 987 AD even most of this remnant population was gone. There are indications that sporadic ceremonial visits may have occurred but eventually the jungle took over, and Tikal was silent until looters, archeologists, and tourists came to visit.

The later structures and artifacts at Tikal show the influence of other Indian tribes, particularly from Mexico. These and other facts indicate the large amount of trade and warfare that went on over the centuries between the various groups. Tikal was definitely not an isolated kingdom.

After several centuries of interaction with the Mexican tribes, the rulers of Tikal appeared to reject the influence of the Aztecs and others. This occurred around 700 AD when the great Mexican site of Teotihuacan was destroyed. For Tikal, there was a revival of purely Mayan forms in the art of that period.

As previously mentioned, the constructors of buildings and temples in Tikal frequently built their structures on the tops of other structures. Most of the time they would

---

not simply build over an existing structure but would first demolish the earlier one. This method provided fill for their subsequent edifice.

We had a different guide for Tikal. His name was Foster and his knowledge of the Mayans was remarkable. He explained the details of the Mayan culture as we walked to the various areas.

Tikal is like an iceberg in that the bulk of it remains below the surface. There are some 3,000 structures in this park but only about 300 of them have been excavated. There is no excavation work being done at the present time nor is any planned, as both scientists and the government of Guatemala are concentrating on excavating some of the other sites that abound in the country.

Tikal contains, in addition to the four huge temples, multi-leveled palaces, ball courts, plazas, smaller temples, terraces, shrines, and carvings. The Great Plaza is a remarkable place. It covers an area of about two and one-half acres. Temple I and Temple II are at opposite ends of the level grass-covered plain. To the north is the North Acropolis and across from it the Central Acropolis.

In Tikal's hey-day the Great Plaza was its downtown (think New York's Times Square). It is estimated that at one time there were 100,000 individuals living in this Mayan city. One scholar even claims that there were in excess of 425,000 people residing in Tikal at the height of its classic power. One can imagine thousands of people gathered in the Great Plaza to participate and watch a spectacle or ceremony. What kind of event it might have been will be discussed later in this book.

A ceramic museum displays many of the artifacts that have been found at Tikal. Foster did an excellent job of explaining them and putting them in context with the period in which they were created. A stela museum not only contains several stelae but also displays enlarged photographs of the restoration of Tikal, vividly demonstrating the jungle growth that encompassed even the temples before they were rehabilitated. Some of the huge photos there are from the 1880s.

Also on display is a large model of Tikal that gives an overview of the many buildings and other structures that make up this fascinating place.

(Day 7)

After a good pancake breakfast (the allspice syrup was delicious) and a brief visit to the stela museum, we had lunch on the way, we enjoyed the view from a hotel overlooking Lake Peten Itza, one of the largest lakes in Guatemala.

Following lunch we did a little shopping in a cooperative where several local people were doing woodcarving. Next we proceeded onto the island town of Flores. Crossing a causeway we entered this busy little town and found it delightful. Flores is where the last stand of the

Maya in this area occurred. The Spanish conquered them in 1697.

Several of our group walked around the town visiting the local Catholic church and the town museum. This museum has a replica of the Dresden Codex, which is a major Mayan relic. There are four codexes which survived the Spanish book-burning. These are books that record in pictures and writing which gods and what acts were associated with days of the calendar as well as facts about astronomy. They apparently were intended for the use of calendric priests.

The Dresden Codex (so named because it presently resides in the city of Dresden, Germany) is made of beaten-bark paper coated with a fine plaster surface and folded like an accordion. This codex, like the others, was read by folding the leaves from left to right until the end of one side was reached. Then the codex was turned over and the other side read.

Our bus took us through the bustling town of Santa Elena to the airfield where Nathan left us (he was driving the bus back to Belize City.) There we caught a flight back to the International Airport in Belize City. The plane that carried us was a fourteen passenger, single-engine Cessna Caravan. The high wings made it possible for us to look down at the jungle we flew over and, later, the shimmering blue-green waters of the Atlantic Ocean.

The plane landed so that we could go through customs

and immigration and then took us on to San Pedro on Ambergris Caye (am-BERG-ris kee.)

Ambergris Caye is the largest of the several cayes in Belize. It has long been occupied largely by fishermen. Twenty-five miles long and thirty-five miles from Belize City, the caye is now the tourist center of the country.

Belize Yacht Club

We checked into the Belize Yacht Club and had a fine fish dinner in a private dining room. The food and the service were both excellent.

(Day 8)

The next morning was spent snorkeling at Hol Chan Marine Preserve and Shark & Ray Alley. Several of our group chose not to snorkel but instead went out on the water in a glass-bottom boat. Whether we were in or on the water we saw many fish, turtles, and huge manta rays. Some of us also saw sharks. The snorkeling equipment rented to the those who didn't have their own was excellent.

After a lunch of chicken cordon bleu and rum raisin ice cream we went out again this time to an area called Coral Gardens. The variety of corals as well as the colorful fish made for a delightful afternoon.

(Day 9)

Snorkeling off the north end of Ambergris Caye at an area known as Mexico Rocks proved to be quite different. Here we saw barracuda as well as turtles and colorful fish.

Those of our group who did not choose to snorkel were dropped off at a pier toward the north end of the Caye and walked along the beach to another pier where they were picked up after the snorkelers were done. The 'beachcombers' got to see another rustic, but comfortable, resort.

Our afternoon was spent at leisure in San Pedro. It is a laid-back town and pleasant to visit. The afternoon at leisure was welcome after the pace we had been keeping. Walking along the beach afforded a variety of water-related sports: wind-surfing, sailing, boats leaving small piers to go snorkeling or skindiving.

San Pedro is the only town on Ambergris Caye and has long been the tourist center of Belize. 'Long' may be a misnomer as the first real hotel was established in only 1965.

Our dinner that evening was the 'Farewell' dinner. All the meals at the Belize Yacht Club were excellent, but this meal of zucchini soup, barbequed chicken, beans, cole slaw, tortillas, and key lime pie was exceptional. As is usually true of International Expedition tours, the group had come together into a truly bunch of good friends.

(Day 10)

This morning we took off for Belize City and our return to the United States. The plane to Belize City was again the Cessna Caravan.

CHAPTER II

Reefs

The coastal zone of Belize is considered to be the region between the high tide line and the 12-mile territorial sea limit. This constitutes an area that is actually larger than the land area of Belize.

The 185-mile barrier reef is one of Belize's outstanding attractions. It is by far the longest reef in the Western Hemisphere and the second longest in the world (after the Great Barrier Reef of Australia). There are dozens of islets (called cayes) along this reef. The largest and best known of these is Ambergris Caye. There are very comfortable lodgings in San Pedro, the only town on the caye.

Divers (primarily skin-divers but also snorkelers) are warned about the coral reefs. Coral reefs can be likened to rain forests in that they are extremely diverse biologically and very fragile. No one is harvesting coral reefs, but they need protection all the same. They constitute only a tiny percentage (0.2%) of the Earth's seas. Coral reefs

---

are easily damaged by divers, fishermen, pollution from boats, and run-off from the land. Divers are instructed not to touch the corals as even a tiny touch may cause damage that will remain for years.

Some things to remember when entering the water where there are coral reefs: take only shallow kicks with your fins when swimming over coral—deep kicks may create such strong pressure waves that coral can be damaged. The same can happen with sand that is kicked up from the bottom. Coral reefs are living beings and need oxygen to survive. Too much sand on them can kill them. Be careful of swimming too close to coral, as a sudden current may carry you into the coral. Keeping a distance of three or four feet is recommended.

Perhaps the most outstanding part of your visit to Ambergris Caye is a visit to the Hol Chan Marine Reserve. When it was first established in 1987 the local fishermen were concerned that it would limit their fishing grounds and thus would limit their catch. The reverse has proven to be true. The fish are using this protected area as a nursery and the neighboring fishery has actually increased its harvest.

The Hol Chan Marine Reserve (Hol Chan means "little channel" in Mayan) has become a model for marine sanctuaries throughout the world. The first marine reserve established in Central America, Hol Chan is achieving both conservation and economic development simultaneously.

Hol Chan is really a break in the reef that ranges from 20 to 35 feet deep. The break was probably created by erosion when the sea level was much lower and the reef was exposed. This "little channel" returns much of the sea water that comes across the reef. Thus even when surface currents are moving inward through this break in the reef there is usually a strong outbound current—only a few inches to a few feet down.

Under the water about 12 feet in the Hol Chan Marine Reserve is a cave and a favorite spot for fish to gather and thus it is fascinating to watch. There also is a "wreck" (really a sunken barge) where a colony of friendly and curious nurse sharks make their home.

Three other areas snorkeled by the International Expeditions group are Shark & Ray Alley, Coral Gardens, and Mexico Rocks.

While snorkeling you will see a variety of living beings in the water. Sea turtles and stingrays are plentiful but you may also see barracudas and even small sharks. None of these critters is dangerous if left alone. It's not a good idea to try to ride a turtle or ray, or to touch a shark or barracuda.

Ambergris Caye is the main one of the several cayes along the barrier reef. The first people on Ambergris were the Mayans. They routed the Spanish in 1508. The name comes from the blubbery gray substance that develops in the intestines of sperm whales. It is said that ambergris used to wash up on the shores of this caye in large amounts until the whalers virtually eliminated the huge beasts in the late 1800s and the early 1900s.

Pirates hid in the coves of the area in the 1600s, and into the 1700s. Ambergris Caye was little populated before the War of the Castes (1847–1853.) Both mestizos and Mayans fled from Mexico across the narrow channel that separates Mexico and Belize at the northern tip of Ambergris Caye. The Mayans dug this channel some 1,500 years ago as a trade route.

San Pedro was founded in 1848. Futile attempts to farm the caye took place in the next few years, but the caye was in foreclosure by 1873 when it was purchased by the Blake family. They focused on coconut production and did quite well at it. In the 1960s the government forced a purchase of the caye and distributed the land to the islanders.

Today, San Pedro is a resort town but it has a relaxed, laid-back atmosphere that avoids the appellation "touristy." Although it has several hundred hotel rooms, it has no big hotels. Its streets are sandy and residents and visitors alike are friendly and casually dressed.

The Barrier Reef is within about a half-mile of the shore at Ambergris Caye, thus protecting the caye from ocean waves. There may be 200 cayes, most of them inside the reef. Many are uninhabited and no more than tiny patches of sand. The reef shelters them, though.

From the air one can see that the water has a bluish-greenish tinge. This is the shallow part inside the reef. On the outside of the reef the water is deeper and displays a dark royal blue. A narrow yellow line divides the two shades of blue. That is the reef.

The water inside the reef is amazingly clear. The colorful tropical fish, the waving sea fans, and the majestic coral gardens provide a spectacular show for the snorkeler. Not to mention the large fish and the sharks, rays, and turtles.

The reef serves several functions. It protects the cayes as well as the mangrove forests, lagoons, and estuaries along the Belize coast. It also provides habitat for many species of marine life—including threatened species such as marine turtles, manatees, and the American marine crocodile. Plus, of course, it provides a wonderful playground for tourists and divers. The Barrier Reef is one of the preeminent diving spots in the world.

There are four atoll reefs to the east of the Barrier Reef. One is in Mexican waters and the other three are in Belizean water. The three are formed on two tiers of submarine ridges that, in turn, are separated by a deep marine trench.

The reef is made of coral. In 2000 the British journal *Nature* ran an article that claimed that much of the reef was dead because of global warming. This was disputed by Belizean divers. Some coral bleaching did occur in the mid-1990s and again in 1998 because the water warmed, but most of the coral quickly regained its health. In later years the water actually cooled —dropping to the high 70s (degrees Fahrenheit) rather than the usual low 80s.

The coral, although it looks like dead stone, is actually a living wall—made up of millions of organisms. These organisms, known as polyps, survive on tiny sea creatures that float by. The polyps feed only at night, pulling back into the reef skeleton during the day. Blue-green algae live within the skeleton and give off oxygen, which the polyps breathe. In a symbiotic relationship the algae absorb the carbon dioxide given off by the polyps.

The polyps, which are tube-shaped, protect themselves by forming a hard layer of calcium carbonate known as corallite. Colonies of these polyps form the structure of the reef. The coral grow in strange and wonderful shapes that give the different varieties colorful names such as brain coral, staghorn coral, and elkhorn coral.

The reef needs solar energy and chemical nutrients to survive. The nutrients, in the form of organic material, flow into the sea from the rivers and creeks on the mainland and from the cayes. This material is broken down into its chemical derivatives by bacteria, thus providing the nutrients needed by the reef.

The water off Ambergris Caye is clear, warm, and inviting. The fact that a visit here comes at the end of your tour provides a relaxing finale to this wonderful experience.

CHAPTER III

Rain Forest

The rain forest contains an astonishing array of animal and plant life. Its giant trees form a canopy, which is both protective and nourishing. The huge trees and other forms of plant life protect from the violent windstorms and torrential rains. Also the canopy shades the forest underneath—serving as a sort of umbrella and holding in the moisture—thus nourishing the vast variety of forms of life that dwell in the rain forest.

Very little of the land in Belize is under cultivation. The obvious reason for this is that the soil is very poor. But there is more to it than that. The amount of rain varies so much, even in the same location, that both flooding and drought are to be expected.

The chief natural resource of Belize historically has been the forests. From the time of the Baymen in the sixteenth and seventeenth centuries, the extraction of timber has been the focus of the area. At first the product was the logwood tree that was used in England to extract a dye for the woolen industry. Logwood trees were found on the scrubby plains near the coast and were relatively easy to harvest.

By the 1770s, the desired tree became the mahogany, which was used for furniture and ships. Later, the wood was used for railroad carriages.

Mammals

There are some 155 species of mammals in this tiny country. Despite being one of the two smallest countries in Central America, Belize has more jaguars than any other nation. But it's unlikely that you'll see one, however, except in the Belize Zoo. Hunting mainly at night, the jaguar is carnivorous and endangered. This beautiful animal was hunted until the 1980s but is now protected. It needs a large area in which to roam and do its hunting. The jaguar has become the unofficial symbol of Belize—and Belizeans are proud of this cat.

The Community Baboon Society (black howler monkeys are called baboons in Belize), formed in 1985, is considered a model for integrating conservation into community life. Wildlife projects around the world have studied this development. Although the howler monkey exists throughout Central and South America, this particular species, the black howler monkey, is endangered and lives only in Belize.

Coatimundi

Ceiba (World Tree)

The official National Animal is the Baird's tapir (also called the mountain cow). The largest land animal in Central America, the tapir also is rarely seen. It is a peculiar-looking animal with a rounded back and rump, thick neck, and large head. It sports a long, trunklike nose and upper lip and feeds on vegetation.

Animals you are likely to see include the agouti, which looks a little like a rabbit, and the coatimundi, which looks a little like a raccoon. You will see (and hear) black howler monkeys as well as spider monkeys. Both simians live up to their names. Gray foxes and deer are common, and you may also see a peccary (a species of wild pig). There also are a number of other wild animals in sparsely populated Belize.

Birds

Belize is truly a birder's paradise with some 533 species having been recorded. The birder on an International Expeditions' tour can expect to record about 150 different species. The serious birder may want to purchase the book **Birds of Belize** by H. Lee Jones. This illustrated guidebook is very helpful, but the naturalist guides are amazingly well versed in the birds of Belize.

Possibly the most striking bird to be seen in Belize is the keel-billed toucan. The National Bird of Belize, the keel-billed toucan is noted for its great, canoe-shaped bill, colored green, blue, red, and orange. This toucan is about 21 inches in overall length. It is mostly black with bright yellow cheeks and chest, red under the tail, and a distinctive white patch at the base of the tail.

Another spectacular bird is the ocellated turkey. Our group saw this colorful ground bird only at Tikal, but it does exist at other locations. The ones we observed behaved much like peacocks. A number of them walked around near populated areas yet they were not really tame. The ocellated turkey gets its name from the eyelike spots on its tail, but the most striking and beautiful feature is the blue head with orange warts. Its metallic, multi-colored tail is almost iridescent. It truly is a gorgeous bird.

The Jabiru stork is the largest flying bird in the Americas by weight. It may be seen at the Crooked Tree Wildlife Sanctuary and at the Belize Zoo. It grows 4–5 feet tall and has a wingspan of 9–12 feet. It has a white body set off by a black head and beak and a bright red sac at the base of its neck.

Speaking of red sacs, the frigatebird can be seen over the cayes. Not endemic to Belize (the frigatebird exists in many parts of the world) it is nevertheless an interesting bird. A soaring bird, the male has a red sac at the base of its neck which is inflated during mating season to attract females. The female has a white breast, but both sexes are basically black.

Its legs are weak—although it can perch it cannot actually walk or swim. It feeds on fish by stealing from other birds. You may see a frigatebird harass a gull or tern that has a fish in its bill until the fish is dropped and the frigatebird swoops down to catch its meal before it hits the water. The frigatebird could be called the thief of the bird world.

Reptiles

Belize contains some 107 species of reptiles including some poisonous snakes. Be assured that the latter are in remote areas where the tours do not go.

The lizards include iguanas and basilisk lizards. Iguanas are very common while the basilisk (also called the Jesus Christ lizard) is a most interesting species. Its claim to fame is its practice of seeming to walk on water. Actually it is running across the surface of lakes and rivers on its large hind feet with flaps of skin between each toe. The fact that they move quickly across the water, aided by their web-like feet, gives them the appearance of "walking on water." Smaller basilisks can run about 10–20 meters on the water without sinking. Young basilisks can usually run farther than older ones. The so-called "old man lizard" is actually a helmeted basilisk.

You will almost certainly see a Morelet's crocodile. The Morelet's crocodile is a smaller version of the American crocodile. It is usually seen at night, particularly in the New River. Although it doesn't have the ferocious reputation of its larger cousin, it still is wise to keep away from it.

Flowers

The black orchid (encyclia cochleatum) is the National Flower of Belize. This orchid grows on trees in damp areas, and blooms nearly all year round. Its clustered bulblike stems vary in size up to six inches long and carry two or three leaves. The black orchid flower has greenish-yellow petals and sepals with purple blotches near the base. The "lip" (one petal of special construction, which is the flower's showiest) is shaped like a valve of a clamshell and is deep purple-brown, almost black, with conspicuous radiating purple veins.

There are said to be 71 species of orchids with many other colorful and beautiful flowers such as hibiscus, bougainvillea, and heliotrope.

Trees

The mahogany tree is one of the magnificent giants of the forest. Rising straight and tall to over a hundred feet from great buttress roots, it emerges above the canopy of the surrounding trees with a crown of large, shining green leaves.

In the early months of the year, when the leaves fall and new red-brown growth appears, the tree can be spotted from a great distance.

The mahogany tree puts out a great flush of small whitish flowers—the blossom for dark fruits, which are pear-shaped capsules about six inches long.

When the fruits mature they split into five valves, freeing large winged seeds, which are carried away by the wind. They fall on the shaded protection of the forest floor and germinate to begin a new life cycle. The mahogany tree matures in 60 to 80 years.

Mahogany trees are scattered throughout the hardwood forests of the interior. The fact that the mahogany trees are scattered throughout the rain forests means that there is little clear-cutting, which has destroyed so many beautiful forests throughout the world. Timber is still being exported from Belize but it is no longer a significant export product.

Other species of tree include the magnificent Spanish cedars, the ceibas (a tree sacred to the Mayans and called by them the World Tree), and the sapodilla or zapote, and several more. Many flowering trees bloom in the spring.

Chicle, a gum taken from the sapodilla tree, has been an important export since the 1880s. It is used in the production of chewing gum. At one time the Creole chicle buyer for the Wrigley Chewing Gum Company of Chicago was a major political and economic figure.

Compared with many other countries (including the United States) Belize is in a good position ecologically. The manner in which the timber harvest was done has resulted in the fact that much of the original jungle of Belize has been retained. Many of the NGOs (non-governmental organizations) and foreign aid programs have focused on the environment with excellent results. Not surprisingly, there is some controversy about the proper extent of logging in the jungle. In 1993, the government of Belize began granting massive long-term logging concessions to foreign-owned companies. This has aroused the ire of environmentalists.

British settlers exploited the forest for mahogany, beginning around the middle of the 17th century. It was originally exported to the United Kingdom in the form of squared logs, but shipment now consists mainly of sawn lumber.

Approximately one-fifth of the land area of Belize is located in some form of protected reserve.

The fact that eco-tourism has become the number one industry in Belize means that the government and investors as well as non-governmental organizations recognize the importance of preserving this jewel of Central America. Of course, that means a certain amount of development is necessary (tourists have to have places to stay and eat). But Belize will never become like Cancun. The hotels and resorts that are being developed utilize the environment and the investors recognize that the beauty of Belize, both on the ocean and in the jungle, must be maintained.

Sugar cane is grown extensively in the northern part of Belize with citrus tree and banana production in the southern valleys of the country. Rice, beans, and vegetables are also produced. Both dairy and beef cattle are grown, as are chickens and bees.

CHAPTER IV

The History of the Mayans

One of the world's greatest civilizations originated in Central America. Without metal tools, wheeled transport, or beasts of burden, the Mayans were exceptional mathematicians and astronomers. They invented a complex hieroglyphic writing system and a calendar that, in many ways, is superior to the one we use today. They constructed huge temples and many other structures with ornate decorations that are nearly without equal in artistic quality. The ancient Mayans were an industrious, hard-working people who extracted a living from a barren land.

Five decades ago the Mayans were thought to be a peaceful people, but more recent excavations and scholarly research have shown that they were a warlike, often violent, people whose rulers were constantly conducting campaigns to conquer neighboring cities. They practiced slavery and human sacrifice. They existed for perhaps as long as thirty centuries and changed greatly during that time. It is almost ludicrous to speak of the Mayan culture as if it existed in a single era. Like all cultures it changed over time and in different locations.

As was true in other ancient civilizations the ancient Mayans were ruled by kings and priests who had almost unlimited power. The record that has come down to us tells us quite a bit about these aristocrats and their lives. Unfortunately, we know very little about the average Mayan.

Let's review the periods of Mayan history that have been established:

>   Preclassic period—(600 BC–250 AD)

>   Early classic period—(250–448 AD)

>   Middle classic period—(448–682 AD)

>   Late classic period—(682–909 AD)

>   Post classic period—(909 AD until the 16th century.)

The Mayan Empire

The Mayan glyphs are a form of writing used by the Mayans from just after the birth of Christ until a century or two after the Spanish conquest. They appear in writings, on pottery, on buildings, and, most commonly, on stelae.

The Mayan civilization spread over much of Mexico (particularly the states of Yucatan, Quintana Roo, and Chiapas), Guatemala, Honduras, a little of El Salvador, and all of Belize. It existed from centuries before the birth of Christ until the Spanish conquest and, in many ways, was the most advanced civilization the world had seen up to that time. It certainly was the most advanced civilization in the Western Hemisphere.

There is no way of knowing how many Mayans there were, but as many as ten million of their descendants still live in the same area. This is five times as many Native Americans as reside in the entire United States. These modern Mayans identify themselves as such, and many of them practice some of the old rituals and follow some of the old traditions.

Glyphs are pictorial representations of various things. A similar system of writing was also used in ancient Egypt. Glyph groups are glyphs that have been grouped together in a square or oval shape. Generally speaking, glyph groups are simply referred to as glyphs.

Fifty years ago only about 5% of Mayan glyphs could be read. Today the figure is more like 80%. Glyphs constitute one of the most complex scripts ever devised. Some are drawings of natural objects. Others appear to be strictly arbitrary. There are about 800 of them that have been identified. In order to better understand the meaning of a glyph, it is helpful to break it down into its parts.

When a number of glyphs (or technically, glyph groups) occur together they are referred to as a text. This is usually the way they are found on a stela. The glyphs are organized into rows and columns and read from left to right in the row, and top to bottom in the column. However, the number of columns to be read in a row depends on whether there are an even or odd number of columns. Even number of columns:

1	2	7	8	
3	4	9	10	
5	6	11	12	etc.

The reading order of odd numbers of columns is either:

1	4	5		1	2	7	
2	6	7	or	3	4	8	
3	8	9	etc.	5	6	9	etc.

Scholars identify glyphs within a text through the use of coordinates using letters for columns and numbers for rows, as follows:

	A	B	C	D	E
1					
2					
3					
4					

The Spanish were the first Europeans to see Mayan glyphs. Only a few Mayans could read them and, as is well known, the Spanish considered them pagan symbols. These Christians made a concerted effort to wipe out any record of the glyphs.

The extensive glyphs of today exist primarily because the jungle covered over (and thus protected) the many structures and stelae on which the glyphs were carved. The first scholarly interpretation of the glyphs was written in the sixteenth century by a Franciscan friar and Bishop of Yucatan, Fray Diego De Landa. It was called "Account of the Things of Yucatan" and languished in obscurity for nearly three hundred years. Virtually nothing occurred on the subject of the Mayan glyphs until Stephens and Catherwood visited Central America twice between 1839 and 1842. Stephens was a noted American travel writer and Catherwood was an English artist. Among other theories, they hypothesized that the monuments depicted rulers and that the glyphs told of royal history. More than 100 years passed before these suggestions were confirmed.

Several manuscripts were discovered in Europe, including De Landa's. These included the famed Dresden Codex. A codex is defined as a collection of ancient manuscript texts. The interpretation of the Dresden Codex led to stunning breakthroughs in the interpretation of Mayan glyphs. It was much easier to study them in libraries than to travel to the ruins themselves. Yet much remains to be understood.

Many scholars have been involved over the years in the interpretation of the Mayan glyphs. There were many false starts, delaying for decades the accurate interpretation of the glyphs. Scholars working on this problem included archeologists as well as architects, linguists, ethnologists, epigraphers, and others.

Michael Coe writes, "this decipherment is one of the most exciting intellectual adventures of our age, on a par with the exploration of space and the discovery of the genetic code."

The "breakthrough" in the deciphering of the Mayan code was made by Yuri Knorosov, a Russian who had never been to the Western Hemisphere. Serving in the Army of the Soviet Union during World War II, his duties took him into Berlin with the first wave of Russian troops. He found the National Library on fire and managed to salvage just one book. That book happened to be a scholarly tome on Mayan hieroglyphics. Taking the book back to Moscow, along with his four battle medals, the young student returned to Moscow University and eventually studied Egyptology and other ancient civilizations. His doctoral dissertation was a translation of—and commentary on—the aforementioned text by the early Spanish missionary, Bishop De Landa.

After that, Knorosov studied and wrote extensively on Mayan hieroglyphics. His contributions led the way to full (or almost full) decipherment. Due partly to the political tensions of the Cold War, Knorosov's

Blue Morpho butterfly

Ocellated Turkey

Black Orchid

Jabiru stork

Mayan temple

Mayan ball court

Pook's Hill Lodge   Ray Snaddon

interpretations were, at first, not readily accepted by the Western scientific community. Eventually it was indeed recognized that this Russian scholar had, in effect, broken the Mayan code.

To illustrate the complexity of the glyphs, consider that the glyph for "tree," for example, occurs in contexts without any connection to trees. This propensity is similar to the rebus principle in which drawings illustrate similar sounds but entirely different meanings. An example in English is that the drawing of a human eye could mean either the pronoun "I" or an actual "eye." This is just one example of the difficulties involved in translating Mayan glyphs.

Another example of the complexity of the Mayan world is their concept of zero. We mean "nothing" by the word zero. The Mayas, however, have a much deeper and spiritual meaning. To them zero does not mean nothing but rather that counting has evolved up to a higher level. There is even a God of Zero.

The Mayan system of numbers, though, is in some ways simpler than ours. It consisted of only three symbols whereas the system we use consists of ten symbols (0, 1, 2, 3, 4, 5, 6, 7, 8, 9). Even the Roman system contains only seven symbols (I, V, X, L, C, D, M).

The three symbols in the Mayan system are a shell for zero (or completion), a dot for one, and a bar for five. Thus, the numbers from one to 8 are as follows:

.	..	...	....
1	2	3	4

	.	..	...
___	___	___	___
5	6	7	8

Numbers larger than 19 are represented by the same kind of sequence, but a dot is placed above the number for each group of 20. For example, 32 consists of the symbols for 12, with a dot on top of the whole thing representing an additional number for each group of 20. The system can thus be extended indefinitely.

Our system of numbering is based on 10, thus called decimal. The Mayan system, on the other hand, is based on 20, and is therefore called vigesimal. The Mayans had no concept of fractions or decimals.

The Mayan calendar is well known as one of the most efficient and scientifically accurate of the various achievements of this Meso-American culture. It was far more complex and accurate than the system we use and served many more purposes. Probably only the ruling elite had complete knowledge of the calendar. The aristocracy thus could prove to their subjects that they held close communion with the supernatural forces that controlled the cosmos. The calendar was used for a variety of purposes, including astrological divination. It was based on a unit of 20 days, and then 20 of the second order, and continued on in multiples of 20.

Actually, it was not really as simple as that. The Mayans had two different calendars. One was 365 days based on the solar year. The other was of 260 days and was used to determine the festivals of the gods and to predict human destinies. When the two were combined it was called the Calendar Round. The two coincided every 52 years.

The Long Count is also a term you will run into if you research the Mayan empire. This calendar term refers to the time that has elapsed since a fixed point in the distant past.

This could not be calculated by the other two calendars. At one time it was thought that the Mayans believed that the world would end on a specific date, i.e.. December 21, 2012. Scholars no longer subscribe to this theory of what the Mayans believed. The late Linda Schele, a prominent Mayanist, compared it to the odometer in your car rolling over from 999,999 to 000,000. December 21, 2012 is the end of a cycle—not the end of the world.

Ball game

The ancient Mayans played a notorious ball game. Ball courts are located at many Mayan sites, including Lamanai and Tikal. In fact there are three ball courts to be found at Tikal. The game was played on an I-shaped field with either sloping or vertical walls on each side. Those in Lamanai and Tikal are sloping and terraced, probably made that way for spectators. Two teams competed at moving a rubber ball using only their hips to propel it.

The ball reproduced the movement of the stars in the sky and the two opposing teams apparently symbolized the struggle between day and night—or between the gods of the underworld and those of the sky. The object of the game in those places that have vertical walls bordering the game field was to put the ball through hoops placed in the walls and perhaps also on the field itself. A sort of Mayan basketball!

The object of the game at ball courts where the wall is sloping is not clear. Sometimes the game was a type of religious ritual. At other times it was simply a spectator sport with wagers on its outcome.

At the end of the game apparently there was a ritual beheading of a human. Scholars differ on who got beheaded. Some say the captain of the winning team; others say the captain of the losers. One theory is that it was the winners early on in the history of Mayan culture and the losers in the latter days.

Sacrifices

Human sacrifice was a routine part of the Mayan culture. It is clear from the decorations and sculptures that have been found that prisoners of war were frequently the victims. However, there were other victims of sacrifices. At times in the history of the Mayans their rulers were sacrificed because it was believed that they were closer to the gods than the common people.

Thus they could avoid going through the nine levels of the underworld and could proceed directly to join the gods if they agreed to be sacrificed. The Mayans dreaded dying of natural causes because the dead were believed to go into a nine-level underworld. Those dying by ritual sacrifice, on the other hand, went directly to paradise.

In the northern part of the Mayan empire, in what is today the state of Yucatan in Mexico, young girls were apparently sacrificed by being thrown into deep wells. The purpose of this practice is not known. Some sacrifices involved taking the heart out of a living person.

In addition to sacrificing people, the letting of blood was an important ritual, particularly for the ruling class. Men would let blood by cutting or puncturing their penises while women would do likewise to their tongues. This bloodletting probably took place under the influence of hallucinogenic drugs and was a technique for visiting the gods. Blood has been referred to as the mortar of ancient Mayan ritual life.

Religion was an integral part of the Mayan culture—no separation of church and state here. The Mayans believed in many gods (at least 166) and daily life was replete with religious practices. As with other aspects of the culture, religious beliefs varied at different periods and in different locations.

The astronomy of the Mayans was sophisticated. Much of their architecture is related to astronomical observation.

E.g. when standing on top of Temple IV at Tikal on the winter solstice (December 21st) the sun rises precisely over Temple I. This is not a coincidence. This sort of exact astronomical feature occurs at many Mayan sites.

The complexities and the differences of the Mayan culture from modern Western culture are immense. This is part of the reason why it has been so lengthy and difficult a task to understand the language and culture.

Mayan Languages

There are actually many Mayan languages. They originated in the Guatemala highlands 4,000 years ago and subsequently split into 31 distinct languages. Today there are three Mayan languages in use. At Pook's Hill Lodge there are two native young women helping out in the kitchen and dining room who are of Mayan descent, and their language is Mayan. However, they are from different parts of Belize and cannot understand each other!

The two subgroups, called Yucatecan and Cholan, embrace the most literate section of the Mayan civilization. They flourished in the lowlands to the north, and east of the highlands. All of Belize is in this area.

Mayan Chronology

The Preclassic period (600 BC–250 AD) was an era of the construction of some huge pyramids. It was also a time when some rather primitive artwork was made. You will see examples of Preclassic art in the museums at Lamanai and Tikal.

The Classic period (250–909 AD) was the richest and most complex time in Mayan society. Inscriptions from this period tend to be heavy on pictorial elements, particularly deity heads, and light on linguistic features. Some inscriptions are on portable objects, usually pottery, while others are carved out of rocks or in caves. Writing was at its peak during this period, exclusively about royalty and the ruling class. There was no mention of the lower classes or anything about economics. This lack has hampered our understanding of the Mayan culture.

The Classic period also saw the expansion of Mayan cities, both horizontally and vertically. New buildings were built upon old. Inscriptions on glyphs and pottery became increasingly irregular, and non-Mayan influences began to appear. This deterioration of the culture was not true at Lamanai, as the site continued to be inhabited and the culture preserved until the Spanish conquest.

Mayan Regions

The Mayan Empire extends into Mexico, Guatemala, Honduras, and El Salvador as well as Belize. The present-day nations did not exist in Mayan times so the borders are irrelevant to the study of Mayan culture. Scientists think that, despite the language differences, the different regions were probably able to read each other's writing and carving.

Mayan Media

Writing and carving were the two methods of recording text. Most carvings were in limestone, which varies in hardness but much of it is quite soft. Unfortunately, a large amount of the softer limestone carvings have weathered away over the centuries. Even those in contact with the ground have deteriorated to some extent because the salt in the soil has leeched into the stonework.

Many of the decorated stelae you will see are difficult to interpret both because much of the stone has weathered away and because many of the decorations are fashioned in a very stylized manner. Your guide will help you to understand these.

The ones that have been preserved were frequently buried in the earth or sheltered by heavy jungle growth. Several other types of stone were sometimes carved, portable objects usually carved in jadeite. The carved stones were frequently painted with blue, red, green, and yellow pigment. Almost all of this pigment has disappeared.

Carving was also done in wood, shells, and bone. Hammered gold appeared in the Postclassic period and stucco was sometimes used on buildings. Interior walls were occasionally covered with smooth plaster. The materials and techniques used varied with the locations and the periods involved.

The carved stones usually contain both stylized representations of people and things and also glyphs.

The glyphs tell stories and facts, including dates. Most surviving inscriptions are on stelae. Many of the stelae you will see have been moved under shelter, sometimes in museums. The glyphs on stelae and buildings are where we have gathered most of the facts about the Mayans.

In addition to carvings the Mayans did painting and writing. They actually had books. Despite the efforts of the Spanish to wipe out the Mayan culture, some 500 books still survived. Those that exist are written on paper made from the inner bark of the fig tree. The books are not bound but rather written on one continuous sheet, which is then folded. The longest book (or folded sheet) is the Madrid Codex. It is more than seven yards in length.

The Mayans considered the ceiba tree to be the World Tree. The introduction of Christianity to the Mayans by the Spaniards was made easier because of the similarity of the World Tree to the cross. The Mayans believed a single World Tree existed before Creation and was the center of their cosmos.

Many Mayan ceremonies and rituals still take place among the millions of Mayans living today in Central America. Some of them occur in caves. Most of these rites are mixed in with the Christian religion. A Catholic Mass in an area populated by Mayans may well have Mayan elements in it.

Of course there is no first-hand account of an ancient Mayan ceremony of human sacrifice, but here is a fictional account taken from Ray Hanson's book **The World Tree.**

Lamanai, Yucatan Peninsula April 25, 608 CE

Two men stood atop a Maya pyramid located in the plaza of the city-state of Lamanai in current day Belize. One of the men, dressed in the official vestments of the king-shaman, was facing an altar from which the sweet smell of burning tree sap could be detected. A gentle breeze stirred the garnishments attendants had used to beautify the holy World Tree cross that occupied the center of the altar. The name of the king-shaman was Lord Smoking Shell. He was offering the official prayers for the occasion. In one hand he held the battle standard of his city. Beside his other hand lay the green obsidian knife he would use to perform the sacrifice. After completing the sacrificial prayers, the king-shaman turned and faced the second man.

The second man, a captured warrior-ball player, stood with his back to the citizens who had gathered in the plaza to observe the ritual. He did not make eye contact with the king-shaman. Upon the command of the king-shaman, the captured warrior-ball player knelt down on his right knee. He had lost in battle but won the ball game. By those two acts he had sealed his fate. He placed his right forearm against his right knee to stabilize his body.

The king-shaman placed his hand on the warrior-ballplayer's head. He spoke to the citizens in the plaza, telling them how he had led their armies in victories over the neighboring, Maya city-states. He reminded them of their prosperity and the good times in which they now lived, and how the sacrifice of the warrior-ballplayer would please their gods. He reached behind his back and brought the obsidian knife to the warrior-ballplayer's neck. He recited more prayers.

After the head had been severed from his body, the warrior-ballplayer's heart pumped blood out of the severed aorta for just a moment. The king-shaman reached into the severed head's mouth and cut out the tongue. The tongue would carry the prayers of the people of the city-state to their protective gods.

What caused the collapse of this great civilization is a question that has plagued Maya scholars (called

Mayanists) for many years. Many theories have been advanced to explain the extinction of Tikal and of the entire Mayan world. Natural disaster, agricultural failure, environmental degradation, warfare, lower-class revolution, and over-population have all been proposed. It has been hypothesized that the ruling families were decimated by so many human sacrifices. It is believed that, at certain periods, royalty figures were sacrificed. Another theory is that genetic inbreeding reduced the ability of the leaders to rule.

David Webster, who has written a book about this problem, believes that the kingdom of Tikal collapsed from a combination of overpopulation and agrarian failure. The soil is depleted by the slash and burn farming technique practiced by the Mayans. Thus, it appears, at least in Tikal, that the community was simply unable to feed its growing population.

Other kingdoms may have collapsed from other causes. Continued excavation and research will undoubtedly reveal even more information about this ancient, yet sophisticated, civilization.

CHAPTER V

History of Tourism

Prior to the 1950s tourism basically didn't exist in Belize. Apparently the government at the time even believed that tourism would ruin the country. From the 1960s to the mid 1980s tourism could be considered to be in the pre-conservation era while the years since are the conservation period.

In 1952 a committee for Tourism Activities was appointed. The budget was $120 per year—none of which was used. About that time several Englishmen came to Belize to oversee some investment projects. Finding nowhere to stay they invested in the Fort George Hotel. Opened in 1953, this was the first hotel in Belize.

The 1960s saw the sleepy fishing village of San Pedro begin to wake up to tourism. The Holiday Hotel was the first to open there in 1966. It had four rooms. The Belize Tourist Board was in existence but mainly just collected taxes and conducted sporadic training programs. Marketing was by word of mouth.

In 1971 Jacques Cousteau, in his famous ship Calypso, visited the Blue Hole near the Barrier Reef. The resulting international publicity contributed to the growth of tourism in Belize. The number of hotels, dive boats, and other tourism facilities continued to increase.

International Expeditions in 1981 became one of the first tour operators to begin offering ecotours in Belize. They have continued to this day, frequently changing their tour routes and facilities visited as new opportunities arise.

The first real attempt by the government to put a focus on tourism took place in 1990, but it wasn't until 1998, with a change in the government, that tourism was recognized as one of the economic pillars of Belize.

Today tourism is an important job creator and is of considerable importance to the economy of Belize. It is expected that the importance of tourism will continue to increase in the future.

CHAPTER VI

History of Belize

The first humans in Belize were descendants of those who came over the land bridge from Asia, perhaps 20,000 years ago. As these people traveled south, many cultures gradually developed in the Western Hemisphere. It is estimated that before the Spanish conquest in the 16th century there were 25 million people living in what is now Central America. This population declined by as much as 90% in the first century following the conquest. This rapid decline was the result, not only of war and killing, but also of the introduction of European diseases to which the indigenous natives had no immunity. This demographic catastrophe may have been the largest in human history.

Before 7000 BC the bands of humans were small and mobile. They survived by hunting and foraging. Around 5000 BC the people living in Mesoamerica spoke related dialects. The division into many languages and cultures came later and about 2500 BC saw the beginning of the

Maya culture. By about 1000 AD some 400,000 Mayans were living in the area that is now Belize. That is nearly twice as many as the total population of Belize today.

Christopher Columbus sailed through the Bay of Honduras (off Belize) in 1502. He named the bay but never landed in Belize. The name Honduras comes from the Spanish word hondo, meaning deep. The first Spanish in the area came in 1508 when an exploring fleet apparently landed. They may have encountered some Mayans and at that point introduced European diseases to the inhabitants.

The Spanish moved into the Caribbean and Central American regions in the 16th century but never settled in Belize. It was the British who first settled in what is now known as Belize.

Cortez's conquest of Mexico began in 1519 and transformed the whole region. After conquering the Aztec Empire, Cortez turned to Guatemala and Honduras. In 1825 he personally passed through the southwest corner of Belize. He conquered the Yucatan in 1527. While in Belize, Cortez found a few scattered Mayan settlements. Later, in the 17th century, these were resettled by the Spanish into what is presently Guatemala.

In 1531 a Spaniard named Alonso Davila was ordered to establish a base at Chetumal on the Yucatan Peninsula. Chetumal is in Mexico virtually on the Rio Hondo, which is the border with Belize. However, archeologists think that in the sixteenth century it was probably located near the present-day Belizean town of Corozal. If that is true then Davila established the only Spanish settlement in Belize. Attacked by the Mayans, Davila fled by canoe down the coast of Belize.

The Spanish continued for over three centuries to have difficulty controlling the Mayans. The cruelty of both the Spanish and the Indians is well documented. At times the Spaniards set rival Mayan tribes against each other. For instance, when the Tipu Mayans of west-central Belize gave up Christianity and resumed their Mayan religion, a Franciscan missionary in the area took the Tipu headman and eighty others to the Lake Peten area of Guatemala and turned them over to the Itza Mayans. The Itza, who were enemies of the Tipu, killed them all.

The Tipu lived near the present-day city of San Ignacio near the western border of Belize. Lake Peten is near Tikal in Guatemala.

The primary invasion of the Spanish into Belize was from the north—from Yucatan. In the seventeenth century Spanish missionaries from Merida (a Mexican city on the Yucatan peninsula) attempted to convert Mayans. They built churches in Belize, including two in the Lamanai complex which the Mayans burned down.

In southern Belize the Spanish had even more difficulty controlling and converting the Mayans. One of the reasons why the Spanish lost control of Belize is that, with the possible exception of Chetumal, they never established a permanent settlement in Belize. Spanish missionaries came and went in various parts of Belize, leaving behind Indian converts who were instructed to continue converting the "heathen," but they never set up a permanent Spanish settlement.

Many Belizeans seem to be proud of (or perhaps only amused by) the fact that piracy played an important part in the early history of their country.

Piracy in and around the Bay of Honduras apparently began around 1565 and continued for more than 200 years. Not much has been recorded about this era, but here are a few incidents that are known:

According to legend, in 1638 the famous Scottish warrior Peter Wallace established a settlement on the banks of the Belize River. There is no proof of this, though.

In the sixteenth century pirates from various countries hid out inside the reefs from which they preyed on the Spanish ships. Although no one knows for certain, it appears that at least some of the British pirates stopped plundering Spanish logwood ships and started cutting the logwood themselves. This probably occurred in the 1650s and 1660s. The Englishmen lived around the Bay of Honduras and were thus called Baymen.

In 1670 the Treaty of Madrid was signed in which the European powers agreed to suppress piracy. Evidently this suppression was unsuccessful. The notorious pirate known as Blackbeard was plundering ships in the Bay of Honduras during the winter of 1717–18. He had a squadron of five pirate ships when he attacked the British ship Protestant Caesar early in 1718.

In February 1719 a pirate named Charles Vane was cruising south of Jamaica when a violent hurricane struck. His sloop was carried by the storm onto a small, uninhabited island in the Bay of Honduras. The ship was smashed to pieces and most of the crew drowned. Vane survived in a miserable state. After several weeks he was helped by some Indians (perhaps Mayans?) who were visiting the islands to catch turtles. Eventually, he was hanged in Jamaica. His crimes are not recorded.

As early as 1720 the log cutters depended on slave labor to do their harsh work. Slavery, from about 1720 until emancipation in 1833, was an important factor in what was then called the Bay Settlements. Slaves in this area were not used in agriculture, as was true elsewhere in the Americas. Instead, they worked in logging. This difference caused early historians to speculate that their living conditions were superior to slaves' lives elsewhere in the Western Hemisphere. More recently, historians refute this hypothesis. The 1790 census disclosed that 75% of the residents of the territory were slaves, 10 % were whites, and the rest were free blacks. The Mayan Indians were uncounted in this census. By emancipation in 1833 the percentage of slaves in the population had declined to one-half.

The slaves were from Africa, some being shipped directly from Benin, the Congo, and Angola, while others came by way of Jamaica and Bermuda. Regardless of how they came to this area almost all were African-born. Perhaps 80% of the male slaves worked as woodcutters. Logwood is a small tree that grows in clumps on the coast. Thus one or two slaves could cut it. When the trade shifted to mahogany, harvesting became more of a problem.

Mahogany trees were (and a few still are) scattered around the jungles of the highlands. Huntsmen located the trees, then cut and trimmed them. The logs were then pulled by cattle to the rivers and, in the rainy season, floated down to the coast. The gangs of slaves that did this work varied between ten and fifty each. This was in contrast to the larger groups of slaves that worked the plantations in the southern United States. Since the gangs of woodcutters were relatively small, it was easy to supervise them.

Nevertheless, slaves were sometimes treated with extreme cruelty. Since the slaves lived in small, scattered, and remote groups, it was relatively easy for them to escape. The runaways went to the Yucatan, Guatemala, or Honduras, although some formed colonies within Belize. Slave revolts were recorded in 1765, 1768, 1773, and 1820. The slave influx had a huge influence on the development of Belize.

Slavery was abolished throughout the British colonies in 1833. (Thirty years before the Emancipation Proclamation in the United States.) It was replaced by a system of apprenticeship that required former slaves to continue working for their former owners at no pay. Also, slave owners were compensated for their loss of property. Finally, in 1838, the apprenticeship system was eliminated. Even after emancipation British law prohibited ex-slaves from receiving Crown land grants. This served to keep labor cheap. However, not allowing former slaves to become independent farmers helped keep the colony unable to feed itself.

In March 1723 Captain Low sailed into the Bay of Honduras. He encountered a Spanish merchant ship and sailed toward it while flying the Spanish flag. When close to the Spanish ship, Low hauled down the Spanish flag, hoisted the black pirate flag, fired a broadside, and boarded her.

During this period Captain Nathaniel Uring, having been shipwrecked, spent several months among the logwood cutters along the Belize River. He was appalled at their excessive drinking and reported that some of them were pirates. The logwood cutters were hard men eking out a difficult living in primitive conditions. They evidently took time out from their logging to plunder passing merchantmen or Indian villages. There were probably no more than 1,000 men cutting logwood during this time. This figure does not count the slaves, who vastly outnumbered the Baymen.

Logwood trees grow in the coastal plains of Belize as well as in nearby areas. Logwood tree trunks grow to five or six feet in diameter. After being felled, sometimes by charges of gunpowder, the trunks were cut into logs. The bark was then stripped off to reveal the reddish-brown heart of the tree. From this core the red stain, which was used as a dye, was extracted. The European woolen industry used the dye made from this particular wood. This dye was the main reason why the British settled in this area. The wood of the logwood tree also was used for medicinal purposes.

Hard economic times came when substitutes were developed for the dyes made from logwood. This resulted in the price of logwood plummeting from 60 to 100 British pounds per ton to 5 or 6 pounds per ton. The settlers turned to cutting mahogany as their chief source of income. The aforementioned Treaty of Paris had prohibited the harvesting of mahogany but allowed the cutting of logwood. The Baymen ignored that prohibition and this upset the Spaniards.

From 1741 on, the British government stationed on Jamaica appointed Superintendents of Belize. This was done despite the fact that the land was claimed by Spain! The Treaty of Paris, signed at the end of the Seven Years War in 1763, allowed the British to continue to cut and export logwood but it left sovereignty with Spain.

In 1768, Admiral Parry suggested to the British Admiralty that a ship be kept in the Bay of Honduras "to prevent as much as possible murders, frauds and Confusion which are notoriously practiced among the Baymen."

In September of 1779, after Spain declared war on Britain, the Spanish attacked St. George's Caye, a tiny island in the Bay of Honduras not far from Belize City. More than 300 settlers and slaves occupied the Caye at the time. All were taken prisoner, marched to Merida, Mexico, and transported to Cuba where they remained until 1782.

The second Treaty of Paris was signed in 1783. This treaty allowed the settlers to return and limited the cutting of logwood to the area between the Hondo and Belize Rivers. Following the arrival of several hundred more settlers in 1786, Belize was essentially British although that fact was not clear until 1798.

But the logwood trade already was in decline and mahogany had become the main export. A further clarification took place in 1786 allowing the Baymen to harvest timber as far south as the Sibun River. However, they were not allowed to build forts, establish any form of government, or engage in agriculture. Spain was given sovereignty and the right to inspect the settlement twice a year.

The last effort of Spain to assert their sovereignty occurred in 1798 when, on September 10th, they again attacked and, with the help of the British Navy, were defeated by the Baymen. This was a pivotal event in the history of Belize and the anniversary of the Battle of St. George's Caye remains a major holiday.

The larger Spanish fleet was defeated, not only by the Baymen and the British, but also by most of their sailors suffering from the "flux" (perhaps their name for dysentery). Another problem for the Spanish was that they weren't familiar with the shallow passages among the cayes and some of their ships ran aground. The Baymen apparently did fight valiantly even though most of them were log cutters, not sailors. Probably some slaves participated, too.

Mexico, which controlled all of Central America (except Belize), gained independence from Spain in 1821. Then, in 1823, Guatemala, Nicaragua, El Salvador, Honduras, and Costa Rica formed a loose alliance that lasted until 1839 when the five countries became independent.

Belize prospered in the early nineteenth century as Spain's influence continued to decline. During this period Belize City was the chief port for Central America. Before the slaves were freed in 1833, many escaped slaves fled into Guatemala. The Guatemalan government had great difficulty in enforcing their asylum law due to the collusion between British slaveholders and lower-level Guatemalan officials. This led to a certain amount of tension between Guatemala and Belize.

The discovery of gold in California in 1848 led to a decline in the trading importance of Belize. The Gold Rush caused the construction of the Panama railway, opened in 1855. Ships leaving from the Atlantic terminus of the railway seldom stopped in Belize City.

Another factor in the decline of the importance of Belize as a shipping center in the mid-nineteenth century was the fact that the government of Guatemala was relatively stable during this period. Because of that stability the British merchants in Guatemala City were able to make direct connections with Europe.

Ship traffic in British Honduras continued to decline during the last half of the century. The British were not worried by this decline, as the important fact for them was that British trade continued. This tended to be the prevailing attitude as long as the British ruled British Honduras. A sort of "What's good for Britain is more important than what's good for British Honduras."

The Caste War of Yucatan (1847–1853) presented a different problem. During this period (and in subsequent years) the Indians of the Mexican state of Yucatan fought both the Mexicans and the British (and a few American mercenaries). It is reported that the population of Yucatan was halved during this time.

The war, little known to history, was actually a rebellion by the Mayans against their white masters. They very nearly managed to drive the whites into the sea. The Indians basically won the war when their adversaries simply quit and went home. The Caste War has been called the only native revolt in North America that succeeded.

Although a Mexican war, it came close to the northern part of British Honduras where the Hondo River constitutes the border with Mexico. This period of war and general instability resulted in thousands of Yucatecans moving into British Honduras, particularly in the north.

A similar situation has taken place in recent years as many thousands of people have left the war-torn countries of Guatemala, Nicaragua, and El Salvador to settle in stable Belize. It could be postulated that the centuries of British rule have made Belize arguably the most peaceful and stable of the Central American countries.

The Cruzob (a rebel Mayan group) were a barbarous bunch that terrorized the Mexicans around them as well as the British Hondurans who lived along the Hondo River. The three-sided dispute (Mexicans, Cruzob Mayans, and British Hondurans) was confusing. At times the Mexicans and British were allies and at other times they were rivals, if not enemies.

The worst part of this dispute occurred in the Spring of 1858. The Mexican town of Bacalar, on the Hondo River, was attacked by surprise by the Cruzob. Most of the town's inhabitants were massacred. Officials were sent from British Honduras to attempt to negotiate for the lives of the remaining Mexicans. The Mayans had an "oracle" or "speaking cross"—a large cross on an altar of the Bacalar Church that appeared to speak through various means of dissimulation. This oracle offered to spare the lives of the fifty or so Mexican captives if the British officials gave 4,000 pesos. They were prepared to give only 2,500 pesos so the Cruzob butchered with machetes the captives, mostly women and children, and within earshot of the British officials.

For the next few years an uneasy peace prevailed in the area. The Cruzob were, more or less, allied with the British during this period. By the beginning of the 20th century the hostility of the Indians had petered out.

In 1862 the Settlement of Belize began functioning as the Colony of British Honduras. This was mainly a symbolic designation as the British had occupied the area for more than 60 years. During this period Britain negotiated several treaties with Central American nations. The most significant of these for British Honduras was the treaty with Guatemala. This required the abandonment of Guatemalan claims to British Honduras and clarified much of the border between the two countries.

In the 1860s it was realized that timber—which had been the strength of the economy of the country for many years—was no longer a major source of income. Combined with the decline in shipping, British Honduras' prospects looked bleak indeed. Then along came the American Civil War (1861-1865.)

At first the war was a boon to British Honduras as trade with the Confederacy rejuvenated the economy. Belize City, in particular, became a magnet for trade to and from the South. Although Matamoros, Mexico, was the closest port to the South, the fact that it was an inland port handicapped it. Ocean-going ships had to anchor several miles downriver and transport their cargo by smaller boats. Belize City was the next closest port and thus profited considerably from the Civil War.

The United States recognized the potential for contraband activity emanating from Belize City and dispatched a representative there. Unfortunately, that individual (George Raymond) proved to be incompetent. In effect he stood by and watched while "shot, powder, and balls" were shipped to the Confederacy. In all fairness to Raymond it must be remembered that the British were sympathetic to the Rebels and came close to recognizing the Confederate States of America. Also, the residents of British Honduras were rooting for the Confederacy mainly because they were profiting from it.

At the end of 1862, Dr. Charles Leas, an experienced professional diplomat, replaced Raymond. (Raymond was definitely not a diplomat.) Leas succeeded in breaking up the contraband trade. Then in May 1863 the Union succeeded in imposing a naval blockade of the Confederacy. This dealt a severe blow to the economy.

By the end of the U.S. Civil War, the lack of immigrants and the necessity to move the economy towards an agricultural base had reached almost crisis proportions. There were only about 25,000 people living in an area the size of Massachusetts.

The timber industry (primarily mahogany) had suffered for many years due to the depletion of the forests. Added to this decline was the fact that the world market for mahogany was lessened by the increasing use of iron and steel in ship construction.

Another discouraging development was a result of the aftermath of the Civil War. In the years immediately following the war many Southerners left the South for British Honduras. The ex-Confederates who settled in northern British Honduras were uncomfortable with the equality of the races as British Honduras had freed their slaves thirty years before the United States.

Those who settled in southern British Honduras found an untamed wilderness. Many of the immigrants were disappointed in the land and the lack of opportunities for profit. By 1869 more were returning to the United States than leaving it, although the Toledo settlement in southern British Honduras survived for decades.

One of the benefits of this temporary immigration was due to the fact that many of the Americans were sugar planters from Louisiana and Mississippi. They introduced sugar cane growing to British Honduras. Sugar production has become one of the mainstays of the Belizean economy.

In September 1872 the last in a series of Icaiche Indian raids took place in the town of Orange Walk. These Indians were based in Mexico, and during the late 1860s and early 1870s had repeatedly raided British Honduras. In one of these raids hostages were taken and a ransom demand was sent to Belize City. This motivated the governor to dispatch a group of soldiers under the command of a British officer. The two groups met, and after a few rounds were fired the British sounded a retreat. The Indians thought that was a call for reinforcements and retreated as fast as they could. So both sides ran away from the field of battle at the same time. History does not record what happened to the hostages.

A new constitution was promulgated in 1871 and British Honduras officially became a Crown colony. This change enabled the country to receive more support from England than had previously been the case. But the locals also lost some of their powers of self-government. Trade basically stagnated during the 1870s, although there were two interesting developments. 1) bananas began to be a product of British Honduras and 2) the first call for a railroad was voiced among the people. Belize still has no railroad today.

The 1881 population figures showed a total population of 27,452 with only 375 whites. Of those whites, 271 were males. The whites, mostly Englishmen, were by this time losing control of the country they had run since the days of the Baymen.

By 1885 there arose optimism about the future of the colony. This was best shown by the enthusiastic participation by British Honduras in the New Orleans Exposition of 1885. In effect, this served to introduce the Colony to the rest of the world.

An amusing incident occurred in 1886. Governor Goldsworthy left his position after two years in office. He had become extremely unpopular due to his evident corruption and favoritism to his friends. He had also depleted the treasury from a surplus to a deficit. When he left for England a number of the citizens showed their delight at his departure by throwing stones at the boat carrying him to his ship. Also a couple of boat-based bands circled his ship playing tunes such as "Good Riddance" and "The Rogue's March." A holiday had been declared and Belize City celebrated this scoundrel's departure into the night.

Incredibly, the British later returned this extremely unpopular administrator to the Colony. Goldsworthy served again from 1887 until 1891 and continued his errant ways and his unpopularity. Perhaps partly because of the insensitivity shown by the Crown, the colonials began agitating against London and its dictates. They came close to bloodshed but did not actually resort to violence.

Then, in 1894, British Honduras converted its currency and went on the gold standard. This resulted in disruption to the economy, caused some strikes and riots, and led to a campaign for self-government. Nothing came of this effort—but the push to advertise British Honduras abroad was undermined.

The year 1919 saw the Ex-Servicemen's Riot. In the early years of World War I patriotism was strong in British

Honduras. Two contingents of Creole soldiers left to aid the British in 1915–16. But instead of going to the front to fight the enemy, they were assigned to the Tigris-Euphrates area (present-day Iraq) as common laborers in support of British troops. They were treated as servants, even denied the right to sing "Rule Brittania!"

After being humiliated during the war, the soldiers returned home only to find themselves provided unacceptable pensions. They also were denied entry to the Belize Country Club and other colonial institutions.

Not surprisingly, they rioted. These were hard times in British Honduras and the riot was joined by many others. This riot was significant in the history of Belize because it marked the beginning of popular movements that continue to this day. The anti-Colonial organizing that took place evolved into a black consciousness movement that, in turn, became almost a black capitalist group. Also, from the Ex-Servicemen's Riot of 1919 sprang the beginnings of a labor movement that evolved into the present-day political parties.

The Great Depression of the 1930s devastated the economy of British Honduras. The country had become increasingly dependent on trade with the United States. When the contracts for mahogany and chicle (used in chewing gum) practically ceased, unemployment rose drastically. Then, on September 10, 1931 a terrible hurricane demolished Belize City leaving over 1000 people dead. The British relief response was poor. The combination of economic decline and the devastation from the hurricane left the colony reeling.

By 1934 there were demonstrations, strikes, and riots. Although these had occurred before in the history of Belize this time they were organized, rather than spontaneous, and thus they marked the beginning of the modern labor movement. The British had put down previous riots, but this time the movement had an effect. The Governor responded to the demands by creating some relief work (stone-breaking at 10 cents a day). Also, he authorized the doling out of a daily ration of a pound of (badly cooked) rice at the prison gates.

The labor movement that began in the 1930s had an effect on the political structure of the country. Specifically, the exploitative labor policies of earlier years gave way not only to more progressive labor policies but also to changes in the political power structure. The old-fashioned colonial oligarchy morphed into a Creole-dominated and elected group of decision-makers.

One of the negatives of the increased role of political parties has been the near-demise of the fajina system. Fajinas are work parties in which people in a community voluntarily come together to work cooperatively on some community project.

At present, and for many years past, Belize has been aided by NGOs (non-governmental organizations) and by aid from number of foreign countries. Some Belizeans have been critical of the extent of the aid received as they feel that it creates a dependency that is not good for Belize. Despite these criticisms, it is certainly true that the various aid programs have been of considerable benefit to the country.

Guatemala and British Honduras

The only country that historically has had a vital interest in the Colony (and now independent nation of Belize) is Guatemala. This fact is due primarily to geography. Guatemala, particularly its Department of Peten (which includes the magnificent Mayan ruins at Tikal), is somewhat dependent upon Belize for transporting its products to the sea. Through Belize City is the most direct route. Geographically, Peten and Belize are a unit. The border between the two is an artificial line drawn through the jungle by a surveyor.

The Guatemalan government was resentful of the British presence in Central America and this has carried over, even since Belize became independent. The Anglo-Guatemalan Treaty of 1859 was viewed by the British as a simple boundary treaty, but by the Guatemalans as a disguised ceding. One provision of the treaty stated that the two governments were to cooperate on the construction of a road from Guatemala City to the Atlantic (presumably at Belize City). Details of how this cooperation was to work were unclear and interpreted differently by the two countries.

This disagreement lasted for many years and never has come to a satisfactory conclusion. Meanwhile, the Guatemalans continued to claim that the treaty of 1859 treated them unfairly. One of the problems was that the situation was that of like a minnow dealing with a whale —little Guatemala negotiating with the huge British Empire.

The Guatemalans thought they were being taken advantage of and the British more or less ignored the situation, as British Honduras was one of their least important colonies. The whole affair was complicated by the fact that the United States and Great Britain were in competition for control of a trans-Isthmian canal route. The United States did not appreciate the British being in Central America.

The whole contretemps was made even more difficult by the fact that there was a growing push for the construction of a railroad between Guatemala City and Belize City. Agitation for such a rail line began in the 1870s. Governments, in both countries, came and went as this confusing situation continued. The Guatemalan Constitution of 1945 declared Belize to be the 23rd department of Guatemala.

The railroad was never built—and roads between Guatemala City and Belize City were not developed until the twentieth century. In 1965 Britain and Guatemala agreed that the United States could mediate the dispute. President Johnson appointed a lawyer, Bethuel M.

Webster, as mediator. He produced a report, presented as a draft treaty that proposed giving Guatemala control over Belize's defense, internal security, and external affairs. Belize would almost cease to exist. Understandably, this raised the hackles of the Belizeans who summarily rejected the report. The United States supported the proposals.

A traveler who flies today into Belize International Airport will note that it is named after a Philip Goldson. This politician/newspaperman is noted for his strong denunciation of the United States after this fiasco.

In the subsequent decade, war between Britain and Guatemala almost broke out a couple of times. On one occasion Guatemala began massing troops on the Belize border, and Britain dispatched an aircraft carrier and several thousand troops to Belize. Later, Guatemala rattled swords again and Britain sent a squadron of Harrier jets to Belize. Confrontations between Guatemala and Belize were not always extremely hostile. At one time the Guatemalan and British soldiers set up a net along the border and played volleyball, with each team staying on its side of the border. Scores of the games were published in the British Army newspaper.

At this point the Belizean government, although still technically a British colony, decided to take their case to international forums. At first, most governments supported Guatemala. In December 1975, the first UN vote on the issue was held. Cuba was the only nation to support Belize.

In 1976, Panama expressed support and in 1977 Mexico and some other Latin American countries followed suit. Nineteen seventy-nine saw the overthrow of the Somoza dictatorship in Nicaragua. The Sandinistas came out in support of Belize and thus Guatemala's military dictatorship lost one of its chief backers. The United States consistently abstained on the annual UN vote on the issue.

In November 1980 the UN passed a resolution demanding the independence of Belize before the next annual session of the world body. One hundred and thirty-nine countries (including the United States) voted in favor of the resolution, with none against, and seven (including Guatemala) abstaining.

Another attempt to reach an agreement between Guatemala and Belize was met with disagreement on both sides and resulted in riots. Tensions (although lessened by the passage of time) continue to this day between Guatemala and Belize.

Mexico and British Honduras

This dispute was not the only one to plague British Honduras. Its boundary with Mexico was also a matter of disagreement for many years. At one time (1865) Mexico claimed all of British Honduras as its own. After much diplomatic maneuvering the border between these two countries was fixed before the end of the nineteenth century. This was relatively easy to decide, as there are rivers that constitute almost this entire boundary.

Early on the residents of British Honduras desired independence. The British attitude was simply that they could have it when they were ready for it. The British Secretary of State for the colonies declared in 1961 that Belize had permission to become independent whenever it wanted. Yet it did not become independent until September 21, 1981. The chief reason for the delay was its dispute with Guatemala. The neighboring country was threatening to occupy Belize and the Belizeans wanted the protection of the British in order to prevent that from happening.

Other British colonies became independent in the sixties—Jamaica and Trinidad and Tobago in 1962, and Barbados and Guyana in 1966. Even after independence a British military force was kept (by mutual agreement) in Belize until 1994.

CHAPTER VII

Belize Today

Like the United States, present-day Belize is essentially a country of immigrants. Even many of the present-day Mayans trace their ancestors back to either Mexico or Guatemala. However, there are many other ethnic groups contributing to this melting pot.

The population has increased over the decades from about 10,000 in 1845 to 272,945 (est. July 2004). In recent years the increase in population has been due to two main factors. The wars and instability in neighboring countries have resulted in thousands of refugees flooding into Belize. A second factor has been the dramatic drop in infant mortality and the death rate in general. Life expectancy is now over 67 years and the median age is about 19 years. The birth rate is high and Belize has become a nation of young people.

The dispersal of the various ethnic groups is, more or less, as follows: The majority of the residents of Belize

City are Creole. The cities of Orange Walk and Corozal and the surrounding rural areas in the northern part
of the country are predominantly Mestizo. (Walk is the
Belizean word for grove.) The southern coastal areas are
mostly occupied by Garifunas (Ga-RI-fu-nas) while the
Mayans, Mennonites, East Indians, and others are in enclaves in scattered parts of the country.

The languages are even more diverse than the ethnic
groups. Most Creoles speak English and Creole, while
most Mestizos speak Spanish. Some also speak English.
Garifunas speak their own language but all also speak
English and also understand Creole. Mayas have three
languages (Yucatec, Mopan, and Kekchi.) Mennonites
primarily speak Low German, and many do not speak
any other language.

English is the official language of Belize. One authority
estimates that about 80% of the citizenry speak English.
Many Belizeans are either bilingual or trilingual.

The religious breakdown is as follows:
RomanCatholic 49.6%
Protestant 27%
    Anglican 5.3%
    Methodist 3.5%
    Mennonite 4.1%
    Seventh-DayAdventist 5.2%
    Pentecostal 7.4%
    Jehovah'sWitnesses 1.5%
none   9.4%,
other 14%.

The Anglicans established the first church, and in 1824 it was incorporated into the diocese of Jamaica. Baptist missionaries arrived in 1822, Methodist missionaries in 1825.

The first Catholic Church began in 1851 (not counting the failed efforts of Spanish missionaries in the seventeenth century). Belize became a Catholic bishopric in 1956. On March 9, 1983 Pope John Paul II visited Belize. This was a big deal for the tiny nation even though the Pope never left the international airport. He was greeted by 15,000 people (a huge crowd for Belize). The Catholic religion cuts across ethnic and geographic lines. About half of Belizeans are Catholics and with a significant number of most ethnic groups Catholic, it is clearly the predominant religion.

Independence Day saw a major celebration. Reportedly, one of the many celebratory activities was the planting of a mahogany tree (Belize's national tree) in every village.

Both before and after independence, one of the chief (but subtle) problems of the nation has been to define a national identity. One of the basic questions is whether Belize is a Central American or a Caribbean country. Geographically, of course, it is located in Central America, but its culture and its population is heavily influenced by the Caribbean, particularly the British West Indies. For a long time the Superintendent of British Honduras (as Belize used to be called) was based in Jamaica.

The country is becoming more Hispanic due to the influx of refugees from other Central American countries. Also a factor is the outmigration of Creoles and Garinagus, most to the United States.

In addition to the profound British influence, the sway of the United States has been significant. This is particularly true in the past few years since the advent of television in Belize.

Another basic question still facing the nation might be: "What does it mean to be a Belizean?" There is no national cuisine—although tamales, rice and beans, and fried chicken are very common dishes. There is no national sport—although soccer is very popular and cricket can be found. The diversity found in the geography is also found in the culture, the ethnic groups, and even in the Mayan ruins and artifacts.

Mestizos

About half the residents consider themselves Mestizo, which simply means 'of mixed race.' The mix primarily is of Spanish and Indian with most Indian blood being Mayan. They are immigrants from, or descendants of immigrants from, other Central American countries. Chief among these, historically, has been Mexico but in recent years there also has been an influx of refugees from the war-torn nations of Guatemala, Nicaragua, and El Salvador.

Creoles

A quarter of the people are Creole—meaning descendants of African slaves. Also, some Creoles are descended from other immigrants from Africa and from early British settlers. To confuse matters a bit more, Creole also has a cultural connotation and, to some extent, describes a way of life that is non-Mayan and non-Mestizo. Their social values are derived, not only from Africa, but also from Britain and the West Indies. In skin coloring they vary from fair to very dark. There are even a few Creoles who call themselves "local whites."

In the days of slavery, the British slaveowners commonly took slave mistresses. Their offspring were called "colored" and their fathers freed some of them. These "free colored" (as well as "free blacks") were free but not equal. Their social position was below that of whites and, at one time, they could not become magistrates or jurors, nor could they vote. After 1808 they could vote in public meetings but their property and residence requirements were twice that of whites. A few became educated and wealthy—some even became slave owners themselves—but most were poor. They were a sort of bridge between the two social poles of society —the British masters and the African slaves. It is from this group that many of the present-day Belizean Creoles are descended. They didn't obtain full civil rights until 1831.

Most of those considering themselves Creole are influenced more by Caribbean and British traditions than African ones. Creoles play a major part in the leadership of both national political parties. They control many of the major newspapers and radio stations. A large percentage of civil servants are Creole.

However, there is a small group of Creoles who are strongly in favor of what might be called Black Power. Some of these are believers in Rastafarianism which is a religion located mostly in Jamaica and the United States that believes that blacks are the reincarnation of ancient Israelites, and salvation can only come from their repatriation to the Holy Land of Zion under the reign of a black king. Rastafarians are the extreme fringe of a black consciousness movement that speaks for only a tiny fraction of Belizeans.

The majority of Creoles live in cities, particularly in Belize City. They have been, traditionally, an urban people although some have worked seasonally in the forests. At one time many of the people had been born in Africa, but as they were slaves, the minority British dominated them. The British, particularly in matters of law, language, and religion, influenced the Africans. In turn, the Africans influenced the British, particularly in matters of dress, speech, cuisine, and social relations.

Mayans

The next largest group (10% of the population) is Mayan, many of whom are either originally from Mexico or Guatemala or are descendants of immigrants from those countries. First, let us deal with the modern Mayans. There are an estimated ten million of them in Central America. (For the purpose of the present book southeastern Mexico is considered to be part of Central America.) Perhaps 30,000 of them live in Belize. Of the three main subgroups of Mayans in Belize today, the Yucatec have pretty much abandoned their language for Spanish. But the Mopans and Kekchi have maintained their own languages.

To a certain extent the Mayans have intermarried with people from the other cultures they have encountered, but this seems to have happened less with the Mayans than with, for example, the American Indians.

The modern Mayans continue to identify themselves as Mayans and to practice some of the "old ways" such as the traditional dances. Although today mainly Roman Catholic, many retain some of the beliefs of their forefathers. There are Mayan enclaves throughout Central America, including ten reservations in southern Belize.

The Mayans have been discriminated against since the Spanish conquest. In one of the early censuses, they were not even counted. According to a 1997 book, MAYA ATLAS, they were not allowed to own the land they lived on within the reservations. As a group they are still near the bottom of the socioeconomic ladder although the newly arrived refugees from other Central American countries may be the bottom rung now.

129

Garifunas

Approximately 6% of the population is considered Garifuna. They call themselves Garinagu while their culture and language is described as Garifuna. Descended from three groups—the Carib Indians of the eastern Caribbean, Arawak Indians, and Africans who escaped from slavery as a result of shipwrecks—their language is basically Carib, but their music and dance may be of African origin. Sometimes it is difficult to visually distinguish between Garifunas and Creoles. Despite the similarity between the two Afro-Belizean groups, there is a certain amount of animosity. This is true of all the ethnic groups.

At Christmas time in certain places Garifuna dancers dress in elaborate costumes and perform with drummers in the city streets. The dancers include a king, a clown, and several boys and men dressed as pregnant women. They dance with arms outstretched and mock the white colonizers.

'John Canoe' or 'Junkanoo' is another celebration mixing music and dance. It apparently comes from Jamaica.

Although most Garifunas are Catholic, they maintain their ancestral rite, dugu, which is an expression of their cultural identity. The dugu is a healing ritual that takes place in a dabuiaba, a temple. The ceremony lasts for several days and, in addition to healing, prevents future illness, accidents, and unexplained deaths. Like the

Creoles, the Garifunas have their own language. Living primarily in southern Belize, the Garifunas tend to be fishermen, farmers, or laborers. They also are considered to be fluent in languages and many are teachers or civil servants.

Garifunas came to Belize in the first half of the nineteenth century after being transported to the Bay Islands in the Gulf of Honduras. Earlier, they had resisted British and French colonialism in the Windward Islands of the eastern Caribbean. The Garifunas were defeated by the British in 1796 and 5,000 of them were shipped to the Bay Islands.

From the Bay Islands they migrated to the coast of Central America settling in Nicaragua, Honduras, Guatemala, and southern Belize. More Garifunas came to Belize after a civil war in Honduras. Many worked alongside slaves as mahogany cutters. They were discriminated against in many ways, e.g., like the Mayans, they were not allowed to own land. At one time there were Garifuna reservations as well as Mayan reservations.

The early Garifuna settlers were considered to be fierce fighters and were even believed by some (including Christopher Columbus) to be cannibals.

Mennonites

Mennonites constitute 4.1% of the population or about 10,000 individuals. Their impact on the culture and

131

economy of Belize far exceeds what one would expect from their numbers. Mennonites first came to British Honduras from Mexico in 1958. They purchased a large amount of land (45,000 acres for $100,000 US) and obtained an agreement from the government.

This agreement (called a Privilegium) granted to the Mennonites the right to run their own schools with their own teachers and in the German language. It also exempted them from military service, and allowed them to simply affirm "Yes" or "No" rather than swear an oath when in court. They were allowed to set up their own trust system called the "Waisenamt" with their own rules and regulations. In addition they were to be exempt from any social security or compulsory system of insurance.

In return the Mennonites agreed to bring into the country $500,000 in British Honduras currency and to produce food not only for themselves but also for local consumption and for export. They agreed to obey all laws, including paying taxes.

A similar Privilegium had been granted to the Mennonites by Mexico in the 1920s. The Mennonites are known to be hard-working and good farmers, so they are desirable settlers for countries that have available land and not many people.

Today there are several denominations within the Mennonite community, some speaking only German, having different views of religious doctrinal issues, and differing in their acceptance of modern technology. Generally though, Mennonites dress conservatively in plain clothes and eschew modern technology. They usually drive horse-drawn buggies (although they use tractors on their farms.) My impression is that they seldom smile. Mennonites live together in their own villages or on adjacent farms and have little to do with local people. They have their own schools and churches. Evidently Mennonites are rigid in their expectation that their members not intermarry with other Belizeans.

The different Mennonite communities vary somewhat in their practices and beliefs. There is one community that reportedly owns an airplane and an airstrip. Some maintain the roads through their communities. Most Mennonites keep to themselves but a few actively proselytize. This leads to the surprising fact that there are some Mennonite Mayans!

One of the oldest of the Protestant sects, the Mennonites originated in the German Alps. They moved to northern Germany and to Russia, then to Pennsylvania in 1700. (The Amish are a subsect of the Mennonites). In the late 1800s a group of Mennonites immigrated to Canada. After World War I, some moved to Mexico and to Paraguay. Many years ago they suffered expulsion and even occasional execution, but more recently the groups have moved when governments have restricted their way of life. The group that first moved to what is now Belize came because the Mexican government was trying to include them in the social security system. More about the

Mennonites can be learned from Sawatzky's book **They Sought a Country.**

East Indians

In 1858 about a thousand Indians were brought into the country to work on the sugar estates. They had mutinied against the British army in India and thus were transported to British Honduras. Most settled in the northern part of the country near Corozal where there is still a community named Calcutta.

In the 1870s some East Indians who had been living on islands in the Caribbean began moving into British Honduras. These people already had been in the Caribbean for one or two generations, their forefathers having left the desperate poverty of India. They settled mostly in the southern part of the country in the Toledo district.

This group is unique in all of the Caribbean region in that they lived among Americans rather than English, Spanish, or French. This unusual situation arose because there had been an influx of Americans from the American South shortly after the U.S. Civil War.

The Americans settling in southern British Honduras purchased some 4,000 acres of land in the Toledo District. As their farms prospered, the Americans began hiring East Indians.

Although the Americans allowed the children of East Indians to attend school, they argued successfully against compulsory attendance. This may have been because the landowners needed to have the children in the fields. Americans and East Indians alike worked hard six days a week and then, on Sunday, attended the American-built Methodist church.

Many of the Americans in the Toledo district drifted back to their home country, often selling their land to the East Indians who had worked so hard for them. Some Americans stayed into the 1950s. A few of the older East Indians remember the Americans, and their memories are mostly good. Although the Americans were the employers and the East Indians the employees, they all worked hard under difficult conditions.

Most of the East Indians' cultural heritage, including their Hindi language, has been lost. Although they have retained a few of their traditional foods, they have become so integrated that they seem like Creoles. This is an unfortunate development as this is an ethnic group with a separate identity. An East Indian Council has existed since 1997.

A few East Indians have come to Belize from India in the last fifty years or so, who have not lost their language and culture. They tend to be retailers and many are of the Islamic faith. Mosques now exist in Orange Walk and in Belize City. Travelers in Belize may spot women with the characteristic Muslim garb.

Other Groups

These include the Chinese, many now from Taiwan. In recent years there was a governmental policy (since changed) allowing immigrants to buy Belizean passports. A number of Hong Kong emigrants used this technique to get into the United States. Some who came here with this scheme in mind, however, got no farther than Belize. Many of the Taiwanese have started businesses. Today you will see many Chinese restaurants in Belize.

Evidently, the Taiwan government has taken an interest in Belize and funded a number of projects. Perhaps this is because Belize has recognized Taiwan as an independent country. Or perhaps the recognition came as a result of the money!

Many other nations have provided emigrants to Belize, including the United States, Lebanon, Syria, Germany, and others.

No discussion of religion in Belize would be complete without mention of obeah, which could be classified as "black magic." Obeah is common throughout the Caribbean area, most notably in Jamaica. This African-originated practice is a means of manipulating and controlling the world—both natural and supernatural. Obeahmen are said to have exceptional knowledge of medicines, charms, and fetishes. They also are frequently associated with rebellions. This may have been the motivating factor in the passage of a British Honduras law in

1791 making the practice of obeah a crime punishable by death. Despite this law obeah has continued in Belize and elsewhere although people who practice it may belong to a Christian church. Actually it seems to be more feared than actually practiced.

Music and dancing are important in Belize and have been since the days of slavery. The gombay is both a recreational event and a goatskin drum that is struck with the hand. Christmas, particularly, is a time for the bram, which is a celebration incorporating loud, vigorous drumming and dancing. Creoles have "bruckdowns," calypso-like compositions in which music and words combine to tell a story or to mock a celebrity.

Belizean literature is becoming more distinctive and identifiable as Belizean novels and Belizean poetry are published. This is indicative of the country's growth as a nation. It is interesting to reflect on the parallels between the United States and Belize. Both became independent only after decades of British rule. After less than twenty-five years of independence, Belize could be said to be where the United States was in, say, 1810. This analogy is certainly less than perfect, as Belize is in many ways a modern country with cell phones, traffic jams, and computers. Nevertheless, it is true that Belize is still a recently formed nation.

The feeling of Creole cultural inferiority, which was instilled by the British, has waned. Belizeans today are a proud and nationalistic people. Despite the many, and very different, ethnic groups and their geographic seg-regation, Belize is one country. Its citizens are proud to be Belizeans. They are also proud of the diverse cultural background of its people.

Literacy is estimated at 94% and education is consid-ered to be very important. The school system is better than others in Central America. Historically, the various churches have run schools but the government pays most teacher salaries.

Racial prejudice probably still exists on a subconscious level but there has been very little interracial violence. Political parties and religious groups appear to pay little attention to race.

Belizean Self-Government

Although formal independence was gained in 1981, the country was essentially self-governing for seventeen years before that. From 1964 to 1981 the British retained control only over foreign affairs, internal security, and defense.

The leader of the country during the seventeen years of limited self-government and the first three years of inde-pendence was George Price. His political party was the People's United Party (familiarly known as PUP).

In 1987 the United Democratic Party (UDP) was elect-ed and Manuel Esquivel became Prime Minister. In the

September 1989 elections PUP once again gained control of the government and George Price regained the position of Prime Minister. Price, now an octogenarian and retired, is to Belize what George Washington is to the United States.

The Belize Constitution, which was passed the day before independence, provides for a three-way balance of power similar to the United States. The Governor General, the Prime Minister, and the Cabinet constitute the executive branch of the government. The National Assembly forms the legislative branch. The Judiciary is independent.

Governor General—Appointed by the ruling monarch of Great Britain after consultations with the government and the opposition party this person must be a Belizean citizen. The present Governor General is Sir Colville Young, Sr. He has served since 1993.

Prime Minister—Appointed by the Governor General for a five-year term, he/she is usually the leader of the majority party or majority coalition. Said Musa has been Prime Minister since 1998. As in other parliamentary systems, the PM can call an early election and his government can fall if they receive a "no confidence" vote. This has never happened in Belize.

Cabinet—Appointed by the Prime Minister from legislators of the majority party. There are presently thirteen members of the Cabinet as well as four Ministers

ate. The latter are not members of the Cabinet but
y attend its meetings if invited by the Prime Minister.
Virtually all bills introduced into the National Assembly
originate in the Cabinet. Closed-door meetings always
result in a consensus decision.

The Cabinet members, including the Prime Minister, are
the policy makers for the government. Members are expected to go along with the group's decisions or resign
if they disagree publicly. If they reveal the content of the
discussions they can be prosecuted.

National Assembly—Divided into two bodies, a twen-
ty-nine member House of Representatives and an eight-
member Senate. The Representatives are elected while
the Senators are appointed. Five are appointed by the
Governor General upon the advice of the Prime Minister,
two by the opposition, and one by the Belize Advisory
Council. New laws require the approval of both Houses.

The party in power routinely chooses senators from defeated candidates for the House of Representatives. This
has caused one critic to call the Senate a "House of Re-
jectees."

Theoretically, the House of Representatives is a forum
for debating the issues facing the country, but actually
all the members follow their party's line. The House is
really nothing more than a rubber stamp for the Cabinet,
which has the real power in Belize.

Belize Advisory Council—A seven-person body appointed by the Governor-General on the advice of the Prime Minister after consultation with the leader of the opposition. Its function is to advise the Governor General on such matters as the pardoning of a convicted person. The Chairman is usually a Supreme Court Justice.

Supreme Court—Justices are appointed by the Governor General, are expected to be nonpartisan in their decisions, and cannot participate in political campaigns. Decisions of the Supreme Court can be appealed to the Privy Council in London. This carryover from the colonial days is galling to some Belizeans.

Belize City has a City Council, and several other cities have Town Boards. These have well-defined legal powers. Most villages have Village Councils, which have little legal authority but allow the people to speak.

Politics in Belize is more a matter of personalities than of ideological positions. The two political parties that have governed Belize since its independence have much the same positions. When out of power they tend to be more liberal and when in control of the government more conservative.

About a third of Belizeans live below the poverty line, with the unemployment figure listed at around 9%. Unemployment figures are difficult to compile, though, and it seems likely that there are more unemployed than officially recognized. Although there is no general minimum wage, levels have been established for specific kinds of employment. The Gross National Product (GNP) per capita is $4,900 US. This is more than in Guatemala, El Salvador, Nicaragua, or Honduras.

The history of voting in Belize is interesting. For most of the decades of British rule, voting was not allowed. In 1890 a request was made to allow some members of the governing Council to be elected. The British Colonial Office turned down this request because there were only 400 whites in a population of more than 30,000. Finally, in 1936, the election of five of the thirteen members of the Legislative Council was authorized. The restrictions (income, property, and literacy) on who could vote were so strict that only 1,035 were eligible out of a population of about 50,000.

In 1954 universal adult suffrage became the law. The minimum voting age is eighteen. Universal suffrage was a significant step. From that date on, Belizeans have participated fully in their own political affairs.

A Stable Nation

Historically, as we've seen, Belize has been exploited. For three centuries the reason for its very existence was to produce wealth for Britain, primarily through timber exports. The timber trade—first logwood, and then mahogany—was the mainstay of the economy until the 1950s. Since then there has been a relatively successful effort to diversify. Tourism has been increasingly important, especially in the last few years. Currently it is the primary part of the economy in Belize. An important boost to the economy comes from the money sent home by the thousands of Belizeans living in the United States.

Exports include sugar, bananas, citrus, clothing, fish products, molasses, and wood, while imports consist mainly of machinery and transport equipment, manufactured goods, fuels, chemicals, pharmaceuticals, food, beverages, and tobacco. Because the three major export products are sugar, citrus, and bananas, Belize has been called a "breakfast economy."

One reason that Belize has been (and is) a stable nation in an unstable region is because of British influence. The United States government has not interfered in Belize as they have in other Central American countries. The United States has been nervous about Central America partly because of the importance of the Panama Canal. Until the 1880s the United States had been uneasy with the British being in Central America, but they finally accepted it as a reality.

The influence of the United States has increased in recent years as the influence of Great Britain has declined. Forty percent of Belizean exports go to the United States, while only 23% go to the United Kingdom. As far as imports go, 36% of Belize's imports come from the United States, and only 5% originate from the United Kingdom.

The history of this transfer (from the United Kingdom to the United States) probably can be dated from 1879. In that year the subsidized mail service was changed from monthly service with British Jamaica to fortnightly service with New Orleans. In 1961 the country quit driving their cars on the left (British style) and began driving on the right (American style). In 1976 they changed the currency tie from the British pound to the U.S. dollar. Two Belizean dollars have been worth one U.S. dollar ever since.

Health care has improved dramatically in recent years in Belize. The health care system is good and getting better. The infant mortality rate has declined from 190 per thousand live births in the 1930s to 30 per thousand at present. International aid has assisted in the modernization of the health care system.

A basic social security system was inaugurated in the 1980s. In addition to old-age pensions, it also provides for benefits during sickness, injuries, and maternity.

Trade unions were forbidden by law until 1941 and have been difficult to establish since then because so much labor is seasonal and unskilled. George Price, the founding father of Belize and long-time President, was a union president before he entered politics. Today, labor unions are accepted, but not particularly strong.

The introduction of American television, and, to a lesser degree, Mexican television, has had a widespread effect on the culture. Whether this is desirable is debatable.

Belize has a small volunteer army called the Belize Defense Force. Formed in 1978 the BDF's main functions are border surveillance, anti-drug smuggling activities, defense of the international airport, and assistance to local police. The BDF received aid in its early days from Britain, the United States, and Canada. Its officers are still trained at Fort Benning, Georgia.

Human rights are protected much better in Belize than in its Central American neighbors. Police are even occasionally tried and convicted of abuse, a practice almost unheard of elsewhere in Central America. Before 1989, though, the government had an internal organization called the Security Intelligence Service (SIS). The SIS repeatedly harassed and interrogated political dissidents and community activists. Also, the government actually controlled the media. But in 1989 the SIS was abolished and government control of the media was eliminated.

The Human Rights Commission of Belize has a different focus than do similar bodies that investigate human rights violations in other Latin American nations. Elsewhere the concerns are political repression, torture of prisoners, and denial of the right of free speech. In Belize, on the other hand, the concerns are more about basic economic and social rights as well as domestic violence.

Underpopulation remains a problem. The number of people living in Belize has grown tremendously over the years from under 4,000 in 1835 to 90,505 in 1900 to 272,945 at present. However, that is still only 31 people per square mile. To put that in perspective, in the United States the average figure is 80 per square mile, with the state of Massachusetts having a density of 810 people per square mile.

There is very little land that can be used for raising crops. Thus, it is necessary for the country to continue developing new products that don't need fertile soil. The balance of trade is not favorable. In other words, imports exceed exports (they always have.) The revenue stream from taxes does not equal the national budget. The coming of free trade is frightening to Belize. At present the country has agreements with the European Union and with the United States that enable Belize to obtain preferential terms when selling their products, particularly sugar and bananas. They fear this will end with free trade.

As a small country, Belize is more reactive to the ups and downs of the world economy than is, for example, the United States.

The HIV/AIDS epidemic is worrisome, although it is not nearly as bad as in Africa. Estimates are that 2.4% of the population of Belize is infected. This is the highest of any Central American nation.

Drug abuse, as it is almost everywhere in the world, is a continuing problem—although drug smuggling has been drastically reduced in recent years. Crime, particularly in Belize City, is a concern. A recent meeting of tourism officials discussed the fact that the travel advisory

---

put out by the U.S. Government warned travelers of the high crime rate in Belize City. The tours of International Expeditions do not even go there. Alcoholism remains a major social problem.

The infrastructure has been developed in an uneven fashion. Generally speaking, the telephone system meets the needs of the people but the road system does not. Roads are being expanded, paved, and improved at a rapid clip, however.

Belize is a young country on the move. Its many attractive features combine to provide both a unique and enjoyable destination.

BIBLIOGRAPHY

Archaeology Magazine Editors. *Secrets of the Maya.*
New York and London: Hatherleigh Press,
2003.

Barry, Tom, *Inside Belize*, Albuquerque, New
Mexico: The Inter-Hemispheric Education
Resource Center, 1992 & 1995.

Belize Review, *Issue on Tourism and the
Environment*, July, 1993.

Bolland, O. Nigel. *Belize: A New Nation in Central `
America.* Boulder and London: Westview
Press, 1986.

_____. *Colonialism and Resistance in Belize:
Essays in Historical Sociology.* Belize City:
Cubola Productions, 1988.

_____. *Struggles for Freedom: Essays on
Slavery, Colonialism and Culture in the
Caribbean and Central America.* Belize
City: The Angelus Press Ltd., 1997.

Brennan, Martin. *The Hidden Maya.* Santa Fe, New
Mexico: Bear & Company, 1998.

Carlstroem, Carolyn Miller and Debra Miller. *Belize.*

Melbourne, Australia: Lonely Planet
Publications, 2002.

Clegern, Wayne M. *British Honduras: Colonial Dead
End, 1859-1900*. Baton Rouge, Louisiana:
Louisiana State University Press, 1967.

Coe, Michael D. *The Maya.* Middlesex, England:
Penguin Books, 1966

————. *The Maya.* Fourth Edition. New York: Thames
and Hudson, 1987.

_____. *Breaking the Maya Code*. Revised
Edition. New York: Thames and Hudson, 1999.

Coe, William R. *Tikal: A Handbook of the Ancient
Maya Ruins.* Second Edition. Philadelphia:
University of Pennsylvania, 1988.

Conover, Adele. "Zoo Story." *Smithsonian*, March,
2004.

Cordingly, David. *Under the Black Flag*. New York:
Random House, 1995.

Dobson, Narda. *A History of Belize. Trinidad and
Jamaica:* Longman Caribbean, 1973.

Fodor's staff. *Central America.* New York: Fodor, 2001.

Foster, Byron. *The Baymen's Legacy: A Portrait of
    Belize City*. Belize City: Cubola Productions,
    1987.

Foster, Dr. Byron, Ed. *Warlords and Maize Men*.
    Second Edition. Belize City: Cubola
    Productions, 1992.

Foster, Lynn V. *A Brief History of Central America*.
    New York: Facts On File, 2000.

Freidel, David, Linda Schele, and Joy Parker. *Maya
    Cosmos,* New York: Perennial, 1993.

Gonzalez, Nancie L. *Sojourners of the Caribbean:
    Ethnogenesis and Ethnohistory of the Garifuna*.
    Urbana and Chicago: University of Illinois
    Press, 1988.

Greenfield, David W. and Jamie E. Thomerson. *Fishes
    of the Continental Waters of Belize*. Gainesville:
    University Press of Florida, 1997.

Hammond, Norman. *Ancient Maya Civilization*. New
    Brunswick, New Jersey: Rutgers University
    Press, 1982.

Hanson, Ray. *The World Tree*. Myrtle Creek, Oregon:
    For The Summit, Inc., 2004. (Fiction)

Henderson, John S. *The World of the Ancient Maya*.

Second Edition. Ithaca and London: Cornell
University Press, 1997.

Houston, S.D. *Maya Glyphs*. Berkeley and Los
Angeles: University of California Press, 1989.

International Expeditions staff. *Belize: NaturalHistory
and Archeology*. Helena, Alabama,
International Expeditions, 2002.

Iyo, Joseph-Ernest Aondafe. *Towards Understanding
Belize's Multi-Cultural History and Identity*.
Belize, University of Belize City: 2000.

Jones, H. Lee. *Birds of Belize*. Austin: University of
Texas Press, 2003.

King, Emory. *Belize 1798: The Road to Glory*. Belize
City: Tropical Books, 1991.

Laughton, Timothy. *The Maya: Life, Myth, and Art*.
New York: Stewart, Tabori, and Chang, 1998.

Leslie, Robert, Editor. *A History of Belize*. Belize City:
Cubola Productions, 1995.

Mallan, Chicki and Patti Lange. *Belize*. Moon
Handbooks, Fifth Edition. Emeryville,
California: Avalon Travel Publishing, 2001.

Maya People of Southern Belize, comp. *Maya Atlas:*

The Struggle to Preserve Maya Land in
Southern Belize. Berkeley, California: North
Atlantic Books, 1997.

McClaurin, Irma. Women of Belize: Gender and
Change in Central America. New Brunswick,
New Jersey: Rutgers University Press, 1996.

Moberg, Mark. Citrus, Strategy, & Class: The Politics
of Development in Southern Belize. Iowa City,
Iowa: University of Iowa Press, 1992.

———. Myths of Ethnicity and Nation: Immigration,
Work, and Identity in the Belize Banana
Industry. Knoxville, Tennessee: University of
Tennessee Press, 1997.

Merrill, Tim, Editor, Guyana and Belize, Country
Studies, Washington, DC: U.S. Government
Printing Office, 1993.

Morley, Sylvanus G. and George W. Brainerd. The
Ancient Maya. Fourth Edition revised by
Robert J. Sharer. Stanford, California:
Stanford University Press, 1983.

Montgomery, John. Tikal: An Illustrated History of the
Ancient Maya Capital. New York: Hippocrene
Books, 2001.

Perrins, Christopher, Editor. Firefly Encyclopedia of

Birds. Buffalo, New York: Firefly Books Ltd., 2003.

Ranguy, Bismark, Sr. and Kathryn Staiano-Ross. *Tales from A Forgotten Place*. Lawrence, Kansas: Department of Anthropology, University of Kansas, 2003.

Reed, Nelson. *The Caste War of Yucatan*. Stanford, California: Stanford University Press, 1964.

Reid, Fiona A. *A Field Guide to the Mammals of Central America and Southeast Mexico*. New York and Oxford: Oxford University Press, 1997.

Roberts, David. "Descent Into the Maya Underworld." *National Geographic*, November, 2004.

Sawatzky, Harry Leonard. *They Sought a Country*. Berkeley, Los Angeles and London: University of California Press, 1971.

Schele, Linda and David Freidel. *A Forest of Kings: The Untold Story of the Ancient Maya*. New York, William Morrow and Company, 1990.

Schele, Linda and Peter Mathews. *The Code of Kings: The Language of Seven Sacred Maya Temples and Tombs*. New York: Scribner, 1998.

Shoman, Assad. *Thirteen Chapters of a History of Belize.* Belize City: The Angelus Press Limited, 1994.

Simmons, Donald C., Jr. *Confederate Settlements in British Honduras.* Jefferson, North Carolina and London: McFarland & Company, Inc., Publishers, 2001.

Society for the Promotion of Education and Research: *Globalization and Development: Challenges and Prospects for Belize,* Belize City: SPEAR, 1993.

————. *Independence Ten Years After: Fifth Annual Studies on Belize Conference.* Belize City: SPEAR, 1992.

_____. *Second Annual Studies on Belize Conference,* Belize City: SPEAR, 1990.

————. *Third Annual Studies on Belize Conference,* Belize City: SPEAR, 1990.

Stuart, Gene S. and George E. Stuart. *Lost Kingdoms of the Maya.* Washington, DC: National Geographic Society, 1993.

Sutherland, Anne. *The Making of Belize: Globalization in the Margins.* Westport, Connecticut and London: Bergin & Garvey, 1998.

Webster, David. *The Fall of the Ancient Maya: Solving the Mystery of the Maya Collapse.* London: Thames & Hudson, 2002.

Vogel, Susana. *The Mayas: History, Art and Archeology.*Translated by David B. Castledine. Mexico City: Monclem Ediciones, 1995.

INDEX

ORDER FORM

INTERNATIONAL EXPEDITIONS

Name _____

Address _____

City/State/Zip _____

Phone(H)_____(W)_____

___ I want information about the Belize trip described
     in this book.

___ I want information about the other trips conduct-
     ed by International Expeditions

INTERNATIONAL EXPEDITIONS
One Environs Park
Helena, AL 35080

Phone: 800-633-4734

FAX: 205-428-1714

Web: http://www.internationalexpeditions.com